# COPING WITH SHYNESS AND SOCIAL PHOBIA

'An invaluable resource for anyone who is troubled by shyness or social anxiety and who wants to know what to do about it. As well as being a self-help guide in its own right it also answers questions that sufferers often ask about what types of treatment are available and how to choose the best treatment approach. The review of Internet sites relating to professional organizations and anxiety groups provided is an excellent starting point.'

—*Robert J. Edelman, Chartered Clinical, Forensic, and Health Psychologist and a Fellow of the British Psychological Society*

'Written by internationally recognized experts, this book summarises much of what is known about social anxiety and outlines the various treatment options. Illustrated with numerous case examples. Highly recommended for sufferers, their families, and professionals.'

—*David M. Clark, Professor of Psychology, King's College London*

'In *Coping with Shyness and Social Phobia*, Ray Crozier and Lynn Alden provide an intelligent, up-to-date, and sensitive look at these two common but highly misunderstood emotional conditions. Going beyond just being providers of information, Crozier and Alden combine their many years of academic and clinical experience to offer a variety of strategies for overcoming shyness and social phobia that individuals will be able to integrate into their everyday living experiences to enhance the quality of their lives and the lives of those they know and love. Individuals who know the pains and problems of shyness and social phobia are fortunate to have as a source of social support the sense of dedication and compassion Crozier and Alden offer in this wonderful book.'

—*Bernardo J. Carducci, Director of the Shyness Research Institute at Indiana University Southeast, US*

# Coping with
# Shyness and Social Phobia

## A Guide to Understanding and
## Overcoming Social Anxiety

*W. Ray Crozier* and *Lynn E. Alden*

ONEWORLD

OXFORD

A Oneworld Paperback Original

Published by Oneworld Publications 2009

ISBN 978–1–85168–516–5

Typeset by Jayvee, Trivandrum, India
Cover design by Mungo Designs
Printed and bound in Great Britain
by TJ International, Padstow

Oneworld Publications
185 Banbury Road
Oxford OX2 7AR
England
www.oneworld-publications.com

# Contents

# Acknowledgements

We are grateful to our families for their support while writing this book: Lynn Alden thanks Raymond and Sarah; Ray Crozier thanks Sandra, John and Beth.

We are grateful to Dr Bernardo J. Carducci, Dr Michael R. Liebowitz, the American Psychiatric Association, The Royal College of Psychiatrists and Taylor & Francis Ltd for granting us permission to reproduce copyright material.

# Series Foreword

This series is intended to provide clear, accessible, and practical information to individuals with a wide range of psychological disorders, as well as to their friends, relatives and interested professionals. As the causes of emotional distress can be complex, books in this series are not designed purely to detail self-treatment information. Instead, each volume sets out to offer guidance on the relevant, evidence-based psychological approaches that are available for the particular condition under discussion. Where appropriate, suggestions are also given on how to apply particular aspects of those techniques that can be incorporated into self-help approaches. Equally important, readers are offered information on which forms of therapy are likely to be beneficial, enabling sufferers to make informed decisions about treatment options with their referring clinician.

Each book also considers aspects of the disorder that are likely to be relevant to each individual's experience of receiving treatment, including the therapeutic approaches of medical professionals, the nature of diagnosis, and the myths that might surround a particular disorder. General issues that can also affect a sufferer's quality of life, such as stigma, isolation, self-care and relationships are also covered in many of the volumes.

The books in this series are not intended to replace therapists, since many individuals will need a personal treatment programme from a qualified clinician. However, each title offers individually tailored strategies, devised by highly experienced practicing clinicians, predominantly based on the latest techniques of cognitive behavioural therapy, which have been shown to be extremely effective in changing the way sufferers think about themselves and their problems. In addition, titles also include a variety of practical features such as rating scales and diary sheets, helpful case studies drawn from real life, and a wide range of up-to-date resources including self-help groups, recommended reading, and useful websites. Consequently, each book provides the necessary materials for sufferers to become active participants in their own care, enabling constructive engagement with clinical professionals when needed and, when appropriate, to take independent action.

Dr Steven Jones
Series Editor

# 1

# Is this book for you?

## What is the book about?

Our starting point is that many of us feel extremely shy or anxious in social situations. We wish that we did not feel like this and we would like to change things so that we wouldn't have to feel like this. We might have tried to change in the past but found that it was hard to do so – our fears and concerns seem so ingrained that they are resistant to change.

Perhaps you feel this way about yourself. Or perhaps you see these signs in your husband, wife or partner, your child, or a friend. You wish that you could help them in some way and sense that if you knew something more about these problems you would be better placed to do so. The aim of our book is to provide you with clear and up-to-date information about what is known about social anxieties.

Perhaps you have read about social phobia or social anxiety disorder and wonder what they refer to or how they are different from shyness or lack of self-confidence. Or you read or hear about strong claims being made about cognitive behaviour therapy and wonder if that would be helpful to you or to someone you know. What does it involve? How might it differ from other forms of treatment? Is there any evidence that it is more effective than other treatments?

Or you have followed recent debates in the media about the use of medication for the treatment of social phobia or social anxiety disorder (we will explain these terms shortly). Are drug treatments effective in treatment? Is their use appropriate? One form of medication that has attracted controversy recently is a class of drugs known as the SSRIs (Selective Serotonin Reuptake Inhibitors), which were developed for the treatment of depression but are now routinely prescribed for social anxiety disorder (we discuss this treatment in more detail in chapter 9). You might not be at all sure what these drugs are, how they work, or why they might be thought to have anything to do with, say, feeling nervous about going on a first date with someone you find attractive or worrying about having to persuade your colleagues at work to agree with your point of view.

Sometimes the media describe medication as a 'pill for shyness' or a 'cure for shyness' and this raises many questions in your mind. Is social phobia the same as shyness? How can a medical treatment change my everyday behaviour? And why should my nervousness about dating or my awkwardness in conversation be a medical matter at all? Isn't it just me, the kind of person I am, my personality, not an illness that I suffer from and can get over if I take the medicine? Other newspaper reports have described a 'breakthrough' in science, where it is claimed that a gene for shyness has been discovered, and it is difficult to square the idea that shyness has a genetic basis with reports that it can be treated by drugs or by psychotherapy.

These are all good questions and probably you have many more good questions in mind. We – Lynn Alden and Ray Crozier – are psychologists and in this book we aim to tackle these questions from a psychological perspective. We don't assume any prior knowledge of psychology and we will explain any technical terms that we introduce as we go along.

As psychologists we are committed to the essential role that objective evidence must play in deciding if and when treatments are appropriate and effective. Therefore we aim to support any claims we make by reference to well-executed clinical research studies and we will include enough information to enable you to check things out for yourself. We will have succeeded if we can provide you with sufficient information about shyness and social anxiety disorder that will help you to understand better problems of social anxiety – whether these are your problems or those of someone you know, or whether you have picked up this book simply because you have a general interest in this topic. If you want to seek professional help we should have pointed you in some directions that might be better for you to take than others would be.

## What does the book cover?

Chapters 2, 3 and 4 of the book are concerned with the nature of social anxiety and shyness. We ask what these terms mean. Shyness is a common word in everyday language that conjures up a number of images. Perhaps you think of a shy child, bashful, tongue-tied, and awkward in the company of adults. Or a child who tends to play by herself, who is always at the edge of things, never quite joining in. Or you think of an adolescent, self-conscious, easily embarrassed, blushing when spoken to. Perhaps it is an adult, quiet, monosyllabic, can't think what to say, never meets your eye, reluctant to join in social events. Or another adult, who looks forward to parties and meeting people, but is never at ease, perhaps talking too much or laughing too loudly, maybe drinking too much to keep confidence up. Whatever image you have conjured up, it will resemble the images that most other people have in mind: Shyness is to do with awkwardness and being ill at ease with other people. This raises a number of questions:

- Isn't everybody shy?
- What is the difference between shyness and that other common type of uneasiness – embarrassment?
- Isn't shyness an attractive characteristic?
- Am I shy? Is my shyness the same as that of other people?
- Is shyness a part of my personality?
- Can I become less shy even if I have a shy personality?
- Is shyness an illness?
- Is shyness different from social phobia?
- Can shyness be overcome?

If these questions are of interest to you, then we hope that this is the book for you and that these opening chapters will provide you with helpful answers to *your* questions.

These questions might be of more than interest to you. You might be desperate to find out more about the anxiety – perhaps the panic – that you feel in particular kinds of situations. These situations aren't rare, like encountering a bear in the woods: they are everyday, routine. The thought of eating in public terrifies you. You couldn't cope with an argument at work; or with being criticized – you would brood on it forever. You have never had a boyfriend or a girlfriend because you can't bring yourself to ask anyone out.

It could be someone else's shyness that makes you anxious, your child's perhaps. You look on helplessly as he or she goes through the agonies of shyness, perhaps becoming lonely or depressed.

For some people, shyness is something they rarely think about as being of much relevance to them. Most of us are shy on at least some occasions: we know this and can cope with it. For others, shyness is something that they would change if they could. For yet others, shyness is 'crippling', it prevents them from living the life they want to. When your anxieties are intense and they impede social functioning and reduce the quality of your life, you may well meet the diagnostic criteria for social phobia or social anxiety disorder. This is a recognized psychiatric disorder. Twenty or so years ago it wouldn't have been recognized as such. It might have been regarded as symptomatic of something else, for example, of panic attacks or agoraphobia, but it wouldn't have been thought of as a condition in its own right. No specific treatments were available at that time.

Chapter 5 examines the concept of social anxiety disorder. It explains how the concept has changed over the years. It sets out the diagnostic criteria that have been agreed upon in psychiatry. It reports findings on how common it is in the population. We see that it is one of the most common disorders along with depression and alcohol problems.

The next four chapters deal in more detail with the nature of social anxiety disorder and its treatment. Chapter 6 examines the issue of diagnosis in greater detail. It begins by posing the question: How do you know if you need treatment? It examines some of the factors to take into account when deciding whether treatment for social anxiety would be valuable for the individual: impairment of effective social functioning; extreme discomfort during social events; lack of satisfaction with life; reduced opportunities for enjoyment and happiness. The chapter introduces some of the forms of psychological and pharmacological treatments that have proved to be effective. It gives advice on how you might contact sources of treatment. It discusses factors to bear in mind when choosing a form of treatment or a therapist.

Cognitive behaviour therapy has become established as the principal psychological form of therapy for a range of mental health problems including anxiety. Carefully designed clinical studies have demonstrated its effectiveness. What are cognitive processes and what role do they play in social anxiety? These questions are the focus of chapter 7. This chapter places cognitive behaviour therapy in the context of the identification of the factors that *maintain* anxiety. It explains that cognitive behaviour therapy places particular emphasis on the ways that socially anxious people think about themselves and social events. The chapter draws upon research and clinical observation to discuss what we know about how thinking helps to maintain anxiety symptoms and behaviours. This information helps us understand how the therapy works.

Chapter 8 describes in more detail the procedures of cognitive behaviour therapy. It emphasizes that it is a therapy based on *doing* as opposed to talking or thinking: it is based on practice and experimenting. A key element is that of changing safety behaviours. These behaviours are ways of coping with anxiety which we have developed that seem to us to be helpful but which are counter-productive in the long term. I am silent because I don't want to reveal my inadequacies. This seems to work because I am never challenged and never show myself up. But at what cost? Not only am I denying myself the satisfactions that are to be found in social relationships, I am also forgoing opportunities to learn how to deal more effectively with social situations so that I never have the chance to develop confidence in myself. Also, my belief that I have inadequacies is never put to the test. What if I have been adequate all along? What if people do like and respect me for the person I am? There are similar costs whenever I avoid social situations: evasion only removes problems in the short term and is worth little in the longer term. We trust that this chapter will give you insight into cognitive behaviour therapy and enable you to make an informed choice about whether it would be the best treatment for you if you do decide to seek to overcome social anxiety or to give helpful advice to someone you know who wishes to do so.

Chapter 9 examines pharmacological treatments for social anxiety disorder. No new treatments have been developed specifically for social anxiety. Medications that have been developed for the treatment of depression have been successfully applied to the treatment of social anxiety disorder. The SSRIs are the principal class of drug that has been investigated. Treatments to reduce anxiety including beta blockers and benzodiazepines have proved less effective although they are used for the treatment of short-term anxieties about specific events, for example anxiety about giving a speech. The chapter discusses the benefits and limitations of these classes of drugs. It draws attention to any problems with their use including potential side effects. There is increasing public concern over what is regarded as the over-prescription of antidepressant drugs and their extension to social anxiety disorder; we discuss these important issues.

Chapter 10 focuses on anxiety about blushing. We don't devote a separate chapter to this topic because we believe that it is of special significance or because it is very different from shyness or social anxiety. We do so for three reasons: (1) many people regard their blushing as a problem in its own right and believe that they would not be anxious if only they did not blush as much as they do; (2) we hope to show that the issues raised by fear of blushing are similar to those raised by social anxiety disorder, for example, safety behaviours play a prominent part in the maintenance of anxiety in both; (3) there has been growing interest in treating anxiety about blushing through the use of surgery to prevent facial reddening from taking place. We discuss the issues raised by surgical intervention.

## An overview

You will see that we cover a lot of ground in this short book. We hope that it will be relevant to your concerns and that it will help you to cope with your shyness and social anxiety by:

- providing you with information on what we know about these conditions;
- allowing you to learn about the experiences of people who are shy or who suffer from social anxiety disorder;
- drawing your attention to the forms of treatment that are available, whether psychological or pharmacological;
- discussing the benefits and disadvantages of the various treatment options;
- giving information on how to contact sources of help and support.

# 2

# What is social anxiety?

## The situations that elicit anxiety

Very many people, perhaps all of us, feel uncomfortable in at least some of our interactions with other people, attendance at social gatherings, or participation in public events. Most of us would probably agree on a list of the kinds of situations that cause us the most difficulties – when we meet new people, ask someone for a date, attend social get-togethers where we don't know anyone, speak up in front of a group by, say, giving a speech at a wedding or making a presentation at work to customers or colleagues, attend a job interview, speak to our manager in the office, complain about faulty work, or return unwanted goods to a shop.

These can be difficult situations for many, perhaps most of us. We are nervous about having to do what needs to be done, perhaps we dread these occasions when they come round and we may put off confronting them for as long as we can. So we hang around outside the boss's door, postponing knocking on it as long as we can, or we take advantage of every opportunity to delay the meeting. We chat about the weather and everything else rather than draw the decorator's attention to the quality of work we are not happy with; we go to other shops before we can face entering the one where we want to return the garment that doesn't fit or the DVD player that we found to be scratched when we opened the box at home. The anticipation of these encounters can give rise to unpleasant physical sensations and we might spend a lot of time and energy rehearsing what we are going to say, practising our opening lines, thinking what to say if the decorator tells us that the work is exactly what was asked for, or the shop assistant implies that it was us who scratched the DVD player.

When we're actually in the situation, it might be an unpleasant experience as long as it lasts. We notice ourselves sweating or trembling or we have that horrible sensation of 'butterflies' in our stomach. We find it difficult to find the right words to say, although lots of things we might say race through our mind. Will it sound stupid? Will I reveal my ignorance? By the time we have summoned the courage to utter a remark, the conversation has moved on. We feel ill-at-ease, self-conscious, out of place.

We experience a sense of relief when it is over. Perhaps we are disappointed that we did not stand up for ourselves better or make the points we wanted to make. Into our mind come all the clever things we should have said. We wish we had spoken up more clearly and mumbled less. What did everyone think of us? We imagine that those who were present must regard us as shy or think that we have little to contribute; for whatever reason we believe that we haven't made a good impression and this may make it harder for us to act effectively the next time we meet them.

On the other hand, sometimes, perhaps usually, the situation turns out not to be as awful as we had feared and we overcome our initial nerves and perhaps even enjoy the experience. Yet this might not necessarily help us the next time we encounter a similar challenging situation. We will approach it again with little confidence that we will be able to cope with it and achieve what we want to. This is an experience that is common for public speakers, lecturers, or performers of different kinds. They get very worked up before their performance, imagining all the things that could go wrong. In fact, all goes well and they give a good talk or performance, and the response of their audience is positive. Yet the next time they are to perform, all their fears rise up again. It's as if they can never learn to have trust in their ability and can never acquire confidence in themselves as performers.

Such experiences are not restricted to unfamiliar situations or to events such as attending an interview or giving a public speech that most people would describe as awkward for anyone. Having an issue out with a member of your family, asking a neighbour not to park their car in front of our house, or reminding a friend that they haven't returned a book they borrowed or money we have lent them can be challenging experiences too. Even while we appreciate that even these can be genuinely hard things to do we envy those who do seem able to deal with these challenges quite easily and take them in their stride.

## Recurrent anxieties

There are other difficulties which seem to be more about us than they are about the situation we are in, they are hard because of the person we are. Often we describe these experiences in terms of our shyness – they happen to me because of the kind of person I am:

I found him attractive but whenever I was in his company I was so overcome with shyness that I never knew what to say.

> When I go to a dinner party everyone else seems to chat very easily with one another but the conversations that I take part in always seem to dry up and the person I am talking to turns their attention to the person on the other side of them so that I am left on my own, trying to listen to what they are saying and not joining in. This always seems to happen to me wherever I sit.
>
> When anyone I don't know very well speaks to me I just go bright red. Even if they are being really friendly. I hate it.

'Alice' (this is a pseudonym, not her real name: all the quotations and case descriptions in this book are anonymous to maintain confidentiality) describes her inability to converse with her fellow members of a sports club:

> I felt inadequate. I believed I was too young to say anything that would have been of the remotest interest to these people. I felt awkward as if out of place even though we were all together as we belonged to the same tennis club. When anyone did ask me something I would be so concerned about how to reply that I could feel myself heating up and turning red. I tried to find something else to do so I could break away from the group ... I don't get embarrassed or feel shy with an individual from the group but once the 'gang' is assembled I feel intimidated.

These anxieties are specific to Alice's meetings with this group, particularly, she points out, when all the members are together. On a one-to-one basis Alice can talk easily with the other person. (Perhaps you have noticed this in yourself, you are happily chatting with someone but when another person joins you both, you immediately become tongue-tied, can't think what to say and never seem to find the gap in the conversation where you can join in. It doesn't have to take very much to change a situation from a comfortable one to an awkward one.) Alice doesn't mention whether her discomfort is specific to these meetings with the 'gang' or whether she experiences it in other situations too, but many people do feel embarrassed and shy often and in more than one kind of social situation. Nor does Alice say whether she regards herself as a shy person and her discomfort at the tennis club represents only one demonstration of her shyness – perhaps it shows itself in other places too.

Many of us do think of ourselves as a shy person. Our friends, work colleagues and those who know us may also think of us in this way and perhaps describe us as shy when they are talking about us, or even to our face. Feeling shy in the kinds of circumstances we have described is one meaning of the word shyness. Thinking of someone as a shy person is another meaning of the word. It labels them as a type of person. It does not merely describe an experience which they might have at one time or another, whether or not they are a shy person. People who use the word to label themselves or someone else are making a prediction about future behaviour. When we describe ourselves in this way the prediction can be a self-fulfilling prophecy: believing ourselves to be shy we behave in ways that confirm our view of ourselves.

When we talk about having difficulties with social situations, sometimes we are thinking of specific once-off situations – giving a speech at a wedding, say. At other times we are thinking about recurrent though not necessarily frequent situations, like Alice's meetings at the tennis club. The situation is uncomfortable when we are there but otherwise we might not give social anxieties much thought.

Alternatively, some of us find many everyday occasions difficult – we can talk easily with colleagues at work about work stuff but when there is any social conversation, over coffee or in the pub after work, we feel shy and don't know what to say. We rarely join in a group discussion, are embarrassed and tongue-tied if we are asked a question, and a conversation never seems to get going when we are taking part in it. We can find it particularly hard to join in teasing or banter and it is impossible for us to tell a joke when a group are listening (even if the joke had raised a laugh when we had told it elsewhere).

For other anxious individuals, meeting anybody at all is a problem and because of that they keep to their own company as much as they can. This degree of apprehension can have marked effects on their life, resulting in isolation and loneliness that only serves to maintain their level of anxiety.

In summary, the social situations we encounter can give rise to anxiety: we can be nervous in anticipation of them or during the time we are there. This is something we all share. While we can all be uncomfortable on these occasions some people regard these reactions as more significant than that and consider that they have a serious problem with their social life. It might be the frequency with which anxiety is elicited in everyday life that distinguishes those for whom it is a problem from those for whom it is not. It might be the intensity of the feelings that they have that makes the distinction. It might be the disruptive effect that it has on their life. Or it might be their view of themselves – while others feel anxious often or intensely they do not internalize it to the same extent: they don't see it as down to them. This is something that we look at in more detail later in the book.

## Anxiety, shyness, and embarrassment

So far we have been using the terms shyness and anxiety as if they mean much the same thing. Many (though not all) psychologists regard shyness as a form of anxiety. It is easy to reach this conclusion. The experience that we describe when we talk about feeling shy or being shy is similar to the experience that we describe when talking about anxiety in other contexts. While waiting in the surgery to go in to see the doctor we may sweat, tremble and have butterflies in our stomach. Thoughts race through our mind about what the cause of our symptoms might be. We imagine the worst possible outcomes and our anxiety intensifies. We find it hard to think of anything else, to concentrate on reading a magazine or to converse with anyone else in the waiting room. We have no shyness about meeting the doctor – we may know her very well, even know her socially. It is what she might tell us that gives rise to these thoughts and feelings. Similarly we may be anxious about opening an envelope that contains a report of a medical test we have undergone, for example the results of cancer screening. Or we have to open a letter containing our college examination results. It is not surprising that psychologists regard shyness and anxiety about events that are not essentially social in character as similar experiences. Nor is it surprising that the treatments – whether psychological or medical – for anxiety conditions have been applied to social anxieties.

We discuss the nature of anxiety in more detail later in this chapter and elsewhere in this book. First, it might be helpful to introduce briefly the relation between shyness and another common form of discomfort in social situations – embarrassment. Shyness and embarrassment seem to be similar experiences. They can both be unpleasant. Both involve self-consciousness when we are in the presence of others. The embarrassed person is ill at ease, not certain what to do or say, feels foolish and out of place, wonders what others present think of them. Both shyness and embarrassment can be accompanied by blushing and by symptoms of anxiety. One distinction that is made between the two states is that embarrassment is triggered by specific circumstances and disappears when the circumstances change. The kinds of circumstances are familiar to us all: forgetting the name of somebody you know when you have to introduce them to someone; discovering that you had tucked the back of your skirt into the top of your tights; realizing that you have been talking loudly when other conversations have stopped and everyone hears what you are saying; accidentally entering the restroom reserved for the other sex.

Embarrassment is triggered when something happens that creates a predicament for you. This threatens loss of 'face' in front of other people – you appear foolish or incompetent. It creates uncertainty about what to do next – how to rescue the situation – and this leads to being flustered and feeling awkward. Being embarrassed is literally to encounter a bar or barrier in social interactions. You find it difficult to know what to say or do in order to overcome the barrier and get the conversation going again. It is not unexpected that shyness and embarrassment often accompany one other. The shy person's quietness in conversation or abrupt answers to questions can lead to an awkward conversation with many silences which create embarrassment for others present. The shy person may be embarrassed by his or her inability to contribute appropriately to a conversation. Sometimes it is hard to distinguish the two: Is the red-faced student who has arrived late for a class and has to walk across the room with all eyes upon her feeling shy or embarrassed?

We return to the topic of embarrassment in chapter 3 and chapter 10 and consider its relations to shyness and to fear of blushing.

## The nature of anxiety

It might be helpful here to briefly summarize some of the core elements of anxiety. We have already alluded to several of these elements. Psychologists have analysed the experience in terms of cognitions, physiological responses, and behaviours.

- Cognitions refer to thoughts about the situation, memories of past situations, anticipations of future ones, and thoughts about the self.

- Physiological responses are evidence of the body's activities in preparation for self-protective action to deal with threat. We experience these as dryness of the mouth, palpitations associated with increased heart rate, increased breathing rate, perspiration, trembling, queasiness, and increased need to urinate.
- Behavioural manifestations of anxiety include escaping from the situation, freezing, and incapacity to act. Behaviours include silence, minimizing eye contact with others, and attempting to keep in the background and avoid attention

This analysis helps us to understand anxiety. It also plays a part in treatments for social anxiety disorder as we see in later chapters. Cognitive behaviour therapy focuses on the contents of thought and at thinking processes, how we arrive at judgements about social events. Other treatments involve learning relaxation techniques to counteract the symptoms of anxiety. One such strategy is progressive muscle relaxation where you learn to release muscle tension through a series of exercises that involve tensing and relaxing various muscle groups. Sometimes this is combined with a cognitive approach. As we see, cognitive approaches argue that it is important to modify the thought processes that give rise to feelings of anxiety, including physiological symptoms. Changing behaviours is also a principal aim of psychological therapy. People who are anxious adopt behaviours which are aimed at increasing their sense of security. These actions include avoiding drawing attention to yourself, expressing agreement with others to avoid confrontation or having to contribute further to the discussion, and taking steps to make blushing less visible. Therapists call these actions *self-protective behaviours* or *safety behaviours* and helping people to identify these patterns of behaviour in themselves and to learn how to change them is an important element in cognitive behaviour therapy. Anxiety can also be analysed along various dimensions: its intensity, its impact on your life, and the extent to which you blame yourself for your predicament.

## Dimensions of anxiety

### INTENSITY OF REACTION

Feelings of anxiety vary in their intensity. Think of a scale like a thermometer. Instead of measuring temperature it measures how anxious you feel. You might give a score of zero to feeling perfectly relaxed. You might give a score of 100 if, say, you are overwhelmed by anxiety as in a panic attack. You can then decide what score between 0 and 100 to give various experiences. What score would you give to the following?

1. In a busy shopping mall you discover that the child you are looking after is suddenly nowhere to be seen?
2. You tell your partner that you have forgotten to post the letter as you were asked?
3. You arrive home late at night, no one is in, and you can't find your house key?
4. You are waiting to go into an interview for a job?
5. You are introduced to someone you don't know and you have to make conversation with them?
6. You see in your car mirror that a police car is driving behind you?
7. You are eating a meal in a busy restaurant?

Perhaps most of us would agree in the order of the scores that we would give to these situations. Question 1 might obtain a high score for example. We can readily understand that we will feel more anxious in some of these situations than in others and that some people will feel more anxious in these situations than others will.

Anxiety can be a brief flutter of nerves or it can be an over-whelming numbing experience. When someone says that they are anxious about meeting someone for the first time or dating somebody or eating or drinking in a public place we might want to find out how anxious they feel. Most of us are at least some-what anxious about sitting examinations or visiting the dentist; some of us are overwhelmed with anxiety at the thought of these events.

IMPACT ON LIFE

Yet another dimension of anxiety is the impact that it has on the individual's life. Anxiety can be an irritant, something you wished you did not experience. You believe you would be hap-pier if you did not do so. Yet you can cope with it in various ways. Alternatively, it can be disruptive, making it difficult to function effectively in life. Anxiety about meeting people can lead to loneliness and social isolation. What will be disruptive will depend on the circumstances of your life and the demands that life makes upon you. We all try to arrange the circum-stances of our life to fit in with our aptitudes, interests and pref-erences. The child who is poor at sports avoids games if he has the opportunity to do so. The child who enjoys computer games creates time and space to play them and she resists invi-tations to go out to play with others. The individual who finds it difficult to approach strangers soon gives up the job of sales-person. But he or she can only do so if this course of action is open to them. Thus the student who dreads examinations but who wishes to go to university or to obtain professional qualifi-cations necessary for the career she seeks, for example in accountancy or nursing, has to face up to her fears. If she can-not cope with them, her life will be seriously disrupted and impoverished.

The plot of Alfred Hitchcock's film *Vertigo* hinges on a police detective's fear of heights. Normally this would not have any impact upon his effectiveness as a police officer but on one occasion his panic attack contributes to the death of a colleague. He suffers a breakdown and his guilt disrupts his life until eventually he re-encounters his fear and is forced to confront it. This is fiction and high drama, but there is a lesson to be learned from the story. We can try to hide from our fears and hope that we will be able cope with life by avoiding the circumstances that would evoke them. But this can be a risky way of dealing with fears since the feared circumstances cannot always be avoided.

## SELF-BLAME

Another factor in anxiety is our sense of responsibility for our difficulties. Alice seems to believe that she is responsible for her problems with the 'gang' of tennis players. She attributes the source of her problems to her inadequacy, her belief that she has little of interest to say to the other players. She is intimidated, perhaps because she is younger and less experienced than they are and they seem to have more to talk about. Or the other players know each other quite well and seem to find it easier to chat to one another; they have more shared experiences to draw upon. Alternatively they might be a self-contained bunch or a clique who are not particularly welcoming to newcomers. Perhaps, too, they find her youth challenging in some way.

Whatever the reason, Alice interprets her difficulties as *her* problem, not caused by the attitudes or behaviour of the other members of the group. We will see in this book that this difference in point of view is an important one for understanding and overcoming social anxiety. If you believe that your anxiety is caused by factors outside yourself then you will think about the anxiety differently than if you blame yourself for your difficulties. At the same time you will also think about yourself differently.

This can create what is sometimes called a 'vicious circle' that can be hard to break out of. You believe that your difficulties are due to something in yourself. This negative view of yourself fuels your anxiety. This can lead to avoidance of social situations so that you don't get a chance to learn to overcome your difficulties. In turn this contributes to the kind of awkward behaviour that reinforces your sense of inadequacy.

## Anxiety as a problem

Despite the difficulties that Alice describes, she does not give the impression that her problem is in any way unmanageable or that she cannot cope with it. In contrast, for many other individuals who have problems with their social relationships and think that they are to blame for them, the problems are simply excruciating:

An illness.
A handicap.
A nightmare.
A blight on my life.
It makes my life unbearable.

These quotations are from anxious individuals. They are all expressed in extreme language and this conveys the degree to which many people feel overwhelmed by their difficulties. Indeed, many ordinary routine situations can become terrifying. Eating a meal when other people are in the room becomes unbearable if you have an intense fear that you will visibly tremble while you are holding a knife or fork. Because of your fear of trembling you avoid canteens and restaurants. Speaking to your neighbours makes you perspire or stammer so you arrange to leave and enter your house when they are not in sight. You can never think what to say to a fellow commuter whom you see regularly on the journey to work, so when you see him or her walking ahead of you to the station you hang back so that you can sit in a different carriage or even catch a later train. Anything to avoid having to make conversation.

For highly anxious people, everyday exchanges such as asking for directions or speaking to a ticket collector are not straightforward. They become something to dread and to avoid. All the time they suspect that others are thinking badly of them because of the way in which they are behaving or others will think badly of them if they don't hide their inadequacies. They find their behaviour difficult to change because the symptoms of anxiety are so powerful and they blame themselves for this too. Their sense of worthlessness is heightened because of their belief that these situations ought to be straightforward. They seem to be straightforward for everyone else but them.

Many anxious people have an exaggerated view of how much attention people are paying to them or how visible symptoms such as trembling are. Yet people often don't notice these things and may not be aware of the level of anxiety that is experienced. This can lead them to be unsympathetic and to underestimate the distress and difficulties anxiety causes.

It is not surprising that many people who experience these problems seek professional help. These kinds of problems are encountered so regularly by general practitioners, psychologists,

## Case 1

Mark had suffered from severe anxiety for many years and had been diagnosed with social phobia. He had overcome his fears to a large extent though not completely by participating in a group facilitated by a clinical psychologist. In time Mark became a facilitator of the group. All this time he had managed to hold down a stressful but well-paid job. When he gave a talk on social phobia a member of the audience challenged him. She said that he had a good job and had the confidence to speak in front of an audience so his problems couldn't be that bad. She argued that social anxiety was trivial compared with the 'real' problems that other people have.

psychiatrists and counsellors that they have been identified as conditions and have been assigned labels. Social anxiety disorder, social phobia and avoidant personality disorder are labels that are currently in use and we will explain these in this book and describe and discuss treatments that have been developed for individuals who have been diagnosed with these conditions.

## Prevalence

### The prevalence of shyness

As we discuss in the book, shyness and the various forms of clinically diagnosed social anxiety are common in our society and social anxiety has become, along with depression, one of the most prevalent clinical conditions in contemporary life. For example, the prevalence of shyness in society is demonstrated by research conducted by American psychologist Philip Zimbardo and his associates at Stanford University in California.

Zimbardo surveyed a very large sample of high school and college students asking them whether they considered themselves as shy and whether they regarded shyness as a problem. Over forty per cent of those who answered the questions were prepared to describe themselves as shy, and of those who did think of themselves as shy, sixty-three per cent said that their shyness was a problem for them. That is, nearly half of those who were asked thought of themselves as shy and the majority of them believed their shyness was a problem. If you consider yourself to be a shy person, you are not alone in this. Nearly half of the people you know consider themselves to be shy! A large proportion of them see their shyness as a problem. This was an unexpected finding for Zimbardo and it is surprising to us too. It is surprising because the people we know don't give the impression of being shy. It is safe to assume that it is also unlikely that we give them the impression that we are shy. Certainly they might notice that we are quiet sometimes or hold back in conversation, but doesn't everybody at some time or another?

Subsequent research has shown that shyness is widespread among different age groups and is common in all the countries of the world that have been studied. Research also shows that shy people tend to describe their shyness in largely negative terms and a substantial proportion say that they would seek help to change their shyness if change were possible. We discuss shyness in more detail in chapters 3 and 4.

## The prevalence of social phobia

Evidence of high rates of social phobia in the general population is provided by findings from a large-scale American survey reported in 1994, the National Comorbidity Study. The study was designed to obtain an indication of the prevalence of various psychiatric conditions in the United States. It included a survey of a very large sample of people (over 8,000) across the whole country. This was not a survey of patients but of a representative sample of the general population. Specially trained staff carried out interviews based on psychiatric diagnostic tests including questions related to social phobia. The survey concluded that some thirteen per cent of the sample (more than one in ten people) would meet the diagnostic criteria for social phobia during their lifetime.

While it is difficult to get a clear picture of what this statistic actually means for individuals, the research does tell us that social phobia was the third most common psychiatric disorder in the sample, after major depression (seventeen per cent lifetime prevalence) and alcohol dependence (fourteen per cent). In many cases social phobia was associated with depression and problems with alcohol use.

We can relate the incidence of these problems to the high incidence of mental health problems in the population. The web based charity No Panic (see chapter 6) estimates that up to one million people in Britain suffer from social phobia. It is estimated that there were more than 31 million prescriptions for antidepressants in 2006. Specifically there were over 16 million prescriptions for SSRIs, which include Prozac, a rise of ten per cent on the previous year. As we see in chapter 9, this class of drugs is also prescribed for social phobia.

In summary, a large number of people in the general population report high levels of anxiety about interacting with other people in their daily life. These levels are equivalent to the levels reported by patients who have been diagnosed with a clinical condition. Not all of the participants in the research study would necessarily have sought professional help, implying that the numbers of people who are diagnosed with social phobia is an underestimate of the numbers in the population at large who are extremely anxious about social situations.

## Need to change?

Clearly our book is addressing what is for very many people an intractable problem, often something that they have lived with for many years and that they have found difficult to overcome. They do want to overcome it and we hope that this book will be helpful to them and also to those who are not highly anxious themselves but who know someone who is and would like to understand or help him or her.

Often these problems are labelled as shyness or chronic or painful shyness. At the same time, we would not want to give the impression that there is something inherently wrong with shyness or imply that there is any necessity for shy people to change. Indeed, many people say that shyness is simply part of their identity – part of the person they are – and not something that can be changed readily or even something that they would want to change.

Shyness has very many positive qualities, as we discuss in chapter 3. People who are shy can and do have rich and rewarding relationships with other people and lead entirely satisfying social lives. They can be extremely successful in their professional lives.

It is all too easy to judge behaviour against an image or stereotype of the relaxed, competent 'social success', the person who sets the standards for everyone – what the sociologist Susie Scott has called the 'Competent Other'. There is no such person and there are many different ways to be liked, admired and valued by others. The capacity to like, admire and value others makes a good start in this, and many shy people are attentive to others, are good listeners, are modest about themselves, and so on. Nevertheless, sometimes there are features of their lives that shy people would like to change and we trust that the book will be useful to them in achieving this. The research we describe shows that social anxiety can be overcome, so our message is an optimistic one.

Perhaps some readers will have got this far and wonder why we are making such a fuss about social anxiety. They – indeed you – might read Alice's self-description and other accounts we have introduced and protest that this is what life is like in the new millennium and probably has been for ages. Of course, you might think, we all encounter social situations that make us anxious because that is the nature of the society we live in. How could it be otherwise, given the huge changes in society and in human relationships that have taken place over the past fifty years or so?

We have to learn to cope with these situations in one way or another and it makes little sense to say that individuals with these difficulties have some sort of psychological problem, or even suffer from an illness that can be treated with medication. This is a view that is shared by many psychologists and sociologists and we discuss it in several places in this book. We are conscious of the dangers inherent in labelling people and in conceptualizing different styles of behaviour as 'deficits' or as medical problems.

However, we encounter individuals who are deeply unhappy with their life and who seek to change it. If our book can identify psychological techniques that can empower people, that they can choose freely to apply to their own position in order to try to change their lives in directions of their choosing, then we believe we have an obligation to explain these. Similarly, if we are aware of approaches and techniques that are 'sold' as 'cures' and we believe that the available evidence does not demonstrate their efficacy, we feel obliged to draw this to the reader's attention.

## Summary

This book is about social anxiety. This is often described in everyday language as shyness. Shyness can be a response to particular social circumstances, a response that most of us would make in those circumstances – some situations or some people are just difficult to deal with.

When people are interviewed or fill in questionnaires about shyness they tend to think of it in entirely negative terms, as an unattractive part of their personality or as a handicap that they wish they could overcome. Nevertheless, shyness does not have to be a 'problem'. For many people it is something that they have learned to live with and they can cope with it. Or they see it as part of their personality and they value it as such. For many, it can be a positive characteristic, associated with admirable qualities – although often it is seen as positive only in abstract terms or valued as a trait in anyone else but oneself. Nevertheless, it is important to emphasize that just because you think of yourself as shy it does not mean that you are in need of help because of that. It is unfortunate that the media tend to describe all sorts of social anxieties as shyness and to describe it as if it was an illness.

Social anxiety also describes when individuals are troubled or dissatisfied with their behaviour when in the company of others. They experience these difficulties across a range of situations and they feel that their problems are somehow to do with the kind of person they are. It seems to them that other people cope much better than they do; indeed others seem to positively enjoy these situations, they seek them out and appear to be completely at home in them. Anxious individuals' difficulties are exacerbated when they blame themselves for the predicaments that they find themselves in – when the awkward silences, not being able to think what to say, feelings of embarrassment and blushing, sweating and trembling are down to them. It's their fault.

People can be distressed by these difficulties and often seek professional help. Typically their first contact is with their doctor in their local surgery or health centre. They might fear that the doctor will not take their concerns seriously, and in the past this fear has often been realized. Doctors have also been known to regard shyness as a symptom of anxiety or depression and to prescribe antidepressants or anti-anxiety medication. Since the 1980s, psychiatrists have identified a clinical condition that they have named *social phobia*. (Chapter 5 will explain how this came about.) This condition now tends to be labelled *social anxiety disorder*. Doctors are now less likely to think of social anxiety in terms of depression or panic attacks and to think that the patient shows indications of social phobia or social anxiety disorder. The doctor may refer the patient for more specialist psychological diagnosis or treatment.

It avoids confusion to restrict the use of the labels *social phobia* and *social anxiety disorder* to this technical sense. They represent a diagnostic category, defined in terms of whether an individual meets a specific set of criteria. It makes little sense to try to restrict the use of the label shyness, since this word is in our everyday vocabulary. It will be used just as people want to use it, regardless of what professionals say. It can help us to understand shyness by analysing the everyday use of the word in order to explore its connotations, and we do this in chapter 3. Throughout the book we will not equate shyness with social phobia although clearly there will be considerable overlap between the two terms because they both refer in different ways to the notion of social anxiety.

There is considerable overlap between the concepts. We shall see that there are experiences which are common to shyness as it is typically described and to social phobia as it is diagnosed. It is likely that interventions that have been developed for the treatment of social phobia will also be useful for many shy people. Assuming, that is, that they want to overcome their shyness – they may not want to do so, or they might not think that the benefits it would bring them would outweigh the effort that was needed in order to change.

The next chapters look more closely at the experiences of social anxiety, construed as shyness in chapters 3 and 4 and as social anxiety disorder in chapter 5. In the remainder of the book we will examine various kinds of treatment for social anxiety.

# 3

# What is shyness?

## Shyness, talk, and silence

It is often helpful when thinking about psychological concepts to start with the language that we use to talk about these concepts. Shyness is a word that is very commonly used in ordinary conversation and considering how we do so makes a good start to answer the question 'what is shyness?' We do so in a number of ways. Shyness *describes* how people feel and how they behave. It also *explains* why they feel and behave the way they do. As discussed in chapter 2, shyness can refer to a short-lived experience. For example, we say that we are suddenly overcome with shyness, perhaps when our boss joins our group in the work canteen or we find ourselves in the company of someone we find attractive. In another sense, shyness refers to more enduring aspects of someone's personality, when we say that someone is a shy person. If I hear that you are shy this raises in my mind many expectations about you. I think you are probably quiet in company and you don't push yourself forward. You prefer to read a book at home than go to a lively party. I don't *know* that you behave in this way but the description gives rise to predictions about how you will behave. Of course, these assumptions may be stereotypes and not based on accurate observation.

We also refer to shyness to *explain* why someone behaves as they do: 'She was too shy to introduce herself to him.' 'He never speaks up at meetings because he is shy.' Quietness, avoiding looking someone in the eye, appearing timid or hesitant; these are often the behaviours that give rise to the attribution of shyness. Yet sometimes apparently outgoing and sociable people surprise us by confessing that, behind the extraverted exterior, they are shy really. If people are shy when they say very little and also when they talk a lot, shyness is quite a difficult concept to pin down.

Consider, for example, the British disc-jockey, Chris Moyles who presents a highly successful breakfast radio programme for the BBC, attracting an audience of close to seven million listeners. His popularity is evident by the fact that he is said to have added one million listeners to what had been a declining audience before he took over the programme. He has the reputation of being confident, loud, often rude, highly sociable, and eager to talk with strangers. Yet in his autobiography he writes of his shyness when he is not broadcasting, his quietness, lack of confidence in initiating conversations, and discomfort in social gatherings. People he works with also describe him as shy.

Moyles is not alone in contrasting his apparent extraversion with his shyness. Many actors, comedians, and other public performers say that their performing provides an opportunity to escape from their shyness, even that their choice of profession was an attempt to do so. Performers talk of losing themselves in a role. When they are on stage they are playing a part which has a script; off-stage they have to be themselves. The 'stage' can be any setting that provides a structure and a role, where you don't have to appear 'yourself'.

It is useful to distinguish between shy behaviour and feeling shy. Extraverted, sociable behaviour can obscure an underlying shyness in the sense of lacking confidence in your social abilities or in your 'qualifications' to participate. Conversely, a shy demeanour does not necessarily represent evidence of shyness. We are all constrained whenever we are unsure how to behave in particular circumstances, for example when we attend a formal social gathering for the first time.

Motivation might also be a factor in helping performers overcome their shyness. The great jazz singer Ella Fitzgerald described herself as a shy person, but she claimed never to be shy on stage. In interviews she talked about her shyness and quietness at social gatherings and among people whom she did not know very well as well as her self-consciousness about her appearance. But this disappeared when she was on stage and she lost her shyness. She thought this was because she loved what she did and this helped her to find the courage from somewhere to perform.

## Case 1

> Richard is a successful barrister who holds important positions on the board of large financial corporations. He has reached the very top of his profession which requires him to exercise assertiveness and verbal fluency when he is in challenging social situations: presenting arguments in court and chairing high powered business meetings. Despite his skill in these settings he is extremely shy. He finds it difficult to meet people or to make conversation outside the formal settings he works in. He is uncomfortable in social gatherings with his work colleagues and avoids them as much as he can. The structure that his formal role in court or the boardroom provides enables him to bypass his shyness. But it does not help him overcome his shyness outside these roles.

Moyles associates shyness and quietness and these are closely linked in people's understanding of shyness. A recurrent theme is remaining silent in the presence of others, particularly when you wish you could speak up. Even young children refer to a child's quietness when you ask them whether they think a particular child is shy and what makes them think so.

Of course there's nothing wrong with being quiet; often, as we say, it is a virtue. But if you ask shy people about their quietness, you learn that they are dissatisfied with it. Partly this is because they want to talk more; they enjoy the company of others and they wish that they could contribute more to a conversation. There are other reasons for their dissatisfaction with themselves. Their failure to join in contrasts with how they perceive the behaviours of others who are present – other people seem able to know what to say and when and how to say it. Many shy people see themselves as 'outsiders' in the social world: in it, but not truly part of it.

Also, their silence contrasts with their active participation on other occasions. They know they can be talkative when they are not inhibited by shyness. When they describe how they feel when they are shy they report that they are 'tongue-tied', they cannot think what to say. Many things that they think of saying come into their mind, but they don't utter them. Often by the time all these potential contributions have raced through their mind the opportunity has passed and the conversation has moved on. If they feel that they ought to contribute something – perhaps because of the nature of the topic under discussion – they mentally rehearse what they are going to say. They repeat it over and over to themselves, wondering if it will come out right, imagining what others will make of it. And it is this wondering what others will think that is at the heart of their quietness and their shyness.

When you are shy you are uncertain what to say or do. Sometimes you cover this up with being garrulous – talking a lot, even gabbling. Deep down, you are worried about what others will think of you. More specifically, you believe that what you say will affect the opinion that others have of you. You will show yourself to be inadequate or stupid, or make public that you do not know anything about the topic being discussed. You might also fear that others will find out that you are shy. You believe that you are a shy person, but others will not necessarily know this and you don't want them to know. This immediately creates a conflict. If you remain quiet you are more likely to be seen as shy. But you can't speak up because of the inhibition that your shyness creates.

The silence or stillness of the shy person in company is accompanied by intense mental activity – thinking how you appear to others, mentally rehearsing what you might say, thinking up something to say and then rejecting it because you are unsure about the impression it will create.

Keeping quiet and staying in the background, volunteering little information about yourself, reluctant to express an opinion that might be controversial or different from that held by others present or that might attract criticism or even ridicule. This pattern can be thought of as essentially 'hiding', a defensive style based on fear: fear that people will see you for what you 'really are' and that they will think badly of this 'real' you. This pattern of behaviour can have unwanted consequences for shy people: other people fail to perceive their positive qualities; they are overlooked, not invited to events or thought of when roles are assigned, teams are formed or promotion is under discussion; they may be perceived by others as lacking interest in other people, as being self-centred, rude or unfriendly. We discuss these consequences again in chapter 4, where we consider the experience of shyness.

## Shyness and related concepts

So far we have concentrated on one meaning of the word shyness but shyness overlaps with other concepts and here we consider three of these: modesty, embarrassment and timidity. We also consider whether there is a positive side to shyness. It is useful to think about these concepts in order to clarify the meaning of shyness.

## Modesty

Shyness is associated with modesty, a connection that is apparent if we consider some of the synonyms of modesty: reserve, diffidence, humbleness, unassuming. These are all words that can readily describe shy people; reserve and diffidence are also synonyms of shyness. We think of someone who has a shy demeanour as reserved, retiring and unassuming. In the past these qualities have been valued much more than they are today. The dramatist and essayist Alan Bennett writes with great insight and humour about his shyness in his book *Untold Stories*. He describes the positive value that his parents placed upon shy conduct – not showing off, being seen and not heard, speaking when you are spoken to, and so on. It was regarded as a positive quality for a woman to demonstrate in the presence of other people particularly, perhaps, in mixed company. It was also thought appropriate for children when they are in the presence of adults. Of course, shyness in this sense was related to the roles and social positions that people occupied. Women and children were more constrained in company in the past than they are today.

A shy demeanour can be associated with politeness and good manners, just as lack of reserve and modesty are often associated with arrogance, brashness or brazenness. Unlike shyness, modesty does not have an inherently negative character, as something to be overcome.

### 'SHYNESS DOES NOT BRING ANYTHING EXCEPT GOOD'

A positive sense of shyness is apparent when we consider meanings of the word in other languages which have separate words for different kinds of shyness. For example, Arabic has two words for shyness, *khajal* and *haya*. *Khajal* seems to correspond more closely to shyness as an unwanted quality, a restraint on effective social interaction as we have been discussing until now and as evident, for example, in responses to the Stanford Shyness Survey that we described in chapter 2. On the other hand, *haya* is a more positive quality. It refers to desirable and appropriate behaviour, to the rejection of what is bad and immoral, including shyness about saying something wrong or immoral. It describes, for example, the appropriate way for a child to behave towards a parent or a woman to behave in the company of unfamiliar men. It refers to appropriateness of dress, not merely in the refusal to wear clothing that is revealing of the body but also in the rejection of ostentatious display.

This is tied to the beliefs of Islam. Muslim women frequently choose to wear the veil or headdress – the hijab, which is a head-scarf that covers the head but leaves the face visible, or the niqab, which covers the whole face apart from the eyes. The Koran requires women to dress modestly, to cover their bodies. This is explicitly related to shyness. As the Prophet, Sallallaahu Alayhi Wasallam, said, 'shyness does not bring anything except good ... it is one of the branches of Faith or Belief': shyness is associated with virtue and good character. *Haya* is related to the concept of shyness in English in its connotations of modesty, reserve and good manners, although the English concept does not have the religious dimension of *haya*.

The opposite in English of shyness as humility and diffi-dence is surely something like showing off or being boastful. Shy people do not show off. They are often hesitant to speak up because they are afraid that they might be seen as doing so; a participant in our research, describing her failure to contribute to the discussion in meetings, said that she was 'afraid that someone might think, well, who does she think she is'.

Yet there are similarities between shyness and showing off, in that they share a sense that you are the focus of attention. The show-off is happy to be in that position. When you are shy you are self-conscious and feel that you are the centre of attention, you believe that all eyes are upon you. Why do shy people feel like this? One answer is given by another participant in our research into shyness when she exclaimed that shy people have an inflated opinion of themselves: 'what makes them think everybody is so interested in them!' More likely, it is a consequence of the shy person's preoccupation with being seen to fall short. Focusing on your self as you monitor your behaviour produces a bias where you think that other people are attending to you; we return to this in later chapters on helping people overcome social anxiety.

## The positive side of shyness

The relation between shyness and modesty suggests that shyness has a positive side. As we see throughout this book this is not the common view of shyness. Most people dislike their shyness and many of them would change it if they could. The example from Arabic society suggests that different cultures might have different views on the nature on shyness and there is evidence of this. Some fascinating research is emerging from China which suggests the importance of cultural values in defining shyness. As is well known, China has undergone dramatic social and economic changes in very recent times and it is rapidly emerging as an economic superpower. Over this period there has been a move away from a positive value placed on shy, wary, and restrained behaviours, where shy children are accepted by their peers and are regarded as well adjusted. Where shyness was previously associated with greater popularity it is now associated with less popularity. Where shyness was seen until recently as a sign of social maturity it is increasingly regarded as a sign of immaturity and a lack of competence.

Previously shyness had no connection with depression; now shyness and depression are more likely to go together. It seems that the view of shyness in China is coming to resemble perceptions of shyness that are held in Western societies.

The relations between social structures and shyness are evident when we look at Eastern countries where shyness, modesty, and diffidence are more positively valued than they are in the West. When the South Korean diplomat, Ban Ki-moon, was appointed Secretary-General of the United Nations in 2007 concerns were expressed by Western commentators that he was too modest and unassuming in character to make a successful leader who would be able to implement policies that could be frequently controversial and to deal with the politics of international terrorism, human rights, poverty, and famine. Ban Ki-moon responded that many in the West fail to understand the virtues of modesty and humility and mistakenly equate these with weakness. There is a tendency in Western societies to confuse social confidence and assertiveness with strength of character and to regard shyness as softness and weakness. For example, former President George W. Bush adopted the uniform and stereotypical posture of members of the armed forces in order to convey an impression of strength and resolve. Humility and diffidence would not be styles appropriate for the leader of a superpower.

It is possible that a negative view of shyness is characteristic of modern Western societies because of their emphasis on individualism and individual success and the more fluid relationships that are found among different social groups and people of different social status. Boundaries were much more rigid in the past. For example, people dressed in ways that were appropriate to their gender, social class, and status, and it was illegal to dress in clothing of a social class other than your own. Nowadays women wear trousers, men wear cosmetics, both sexes have tattoos that were once restricted to specific social groups. In general, social divisions are more blurred in forms of appearance. Standards for appropriate behaviour also vary, as illustrated by the current popularity of books about good manners from past eras or the reissue of booklets that were issued to service personnel advising them how to behave when they were off duty in a country other than their own, for example, American GIs in Britain in the 1940s. Rigid boundaries make it easier to deal with other people since less negotiation is involved and forms of greeting, topics of conversation, and so on are regulated and everyone has a 'script' to follow. You are also less likely to have to converse with people who have a very different background from yourself. This removes much of the awkwardness of contemporary life.

Not all Western societies assign a negative value to shyness, as some research recently undertaken in Finland reports. This research compared ideas of the word 'shy' held by American visitors to Finland with those held by Finnish speakers. The visiting Americans thought that Finns were extremely shy and unsociable. Some thought that their shyness represented a clinical problem. Finnish participants did acknowledge that as a people Finns are shy and quiet but they did not associate these attributes with social handicap. Indeed, they emphasized the positive side of shyness: not imposing your opinions on others; not bothering others; not talking just for the sake of it.

Once again, shyness is closely connected with quietness, reserve, and inhibition. There is no disagreement about the behaviours that shyness entails. But those Americans who are visiting another country and who bring their own values to the perception of shy, silent behaviours assume that these behaviours are signs of problems that individual Finns have. They assume this because people in their own country who behaved like this would be thought to have a problem. And those who behaved in shy ways in their own country would be likely to believe that they have a problem. Unless, of course, they were natives of Finland! It is very easy to assume that quiet, inhibited behaviours must mean that there is a problem that is in need of correction.

This research illustrates that there is nothing inherently problematic about shyness. It raises the question whether certain kinds of behaving – a 'natural way to be', as one of the Finnish students describes it, takes on different values in different societies and these values influence whether the individual regards this behaviour in a positive or negative light. This is an implication of the research carried out in China. Could this also be true for individual development? Does a child come to regard his or her quiet, constrained behaviour in a negative light because it is disparaged in that culture? To continue this analogy, might one way to modify shyness be to change cultural values – to change the values of the local society in which the child grows up?

We can list some of the positive qualities that can be associated with shyness. It is quite a long list. Perhaps you can think of more qualities.

- reserved
- modest
- diffident
- self-effacing
- considerate of others
- respectful
- sensitive
- tactful
- discreet
- sincere
- hesitant about saying something inappropriate
- thoughtful
- observant

## Embarrassment

Shyness also relates to being embarrassed. As we briefly described in chapter 2 embarrassment is a state of fluster that we experience when we face a predicament during a social encounter. The kinds of predicaments that occur are well known to us all.

Perhaps you can take the time to recall an occasion when you felt really embarrassed.

- What was it that made you embarrassed?
- How did you feel at the time?
- What gestures and expressions accompanied your embarrassment?
- What behaviours accompanied your embarrassment?
- What, if anything, did you do to cope with your embarrassment?

### WHAT WAS IT THAT MADE YOU EMBARRASSED?

When you described an embarrassing incident you could probably identify a specific event that brought it about. This could be something you said or did. Or it could be something someone else said or did. Often what happens to trigger it is unexpected or accidental and takes you by surprise. The existence of a specific trigger helps distinguish embarrassment from shyness. Embarrassment is a reaction to a predicament that has already taken place whereas shyness is the fear or the anticipation of creating a predicament or of finding yourself in an awkward position. While certain features of a situation will make shyness more likely – meeting someone for the first time, attending a social gathering, speaking up in front of others – there is not necessarily a specific incident that brings about an emotional reaction.

Another difference is that although you feel embarrassed you need not be the person responsible for the incident. You can be embarrassed *by* someone else's behaviour or be embarrassed *for* someone else, for example when you see them make a faux pas. You need not be responsible for the circumstances that lead to your embarrassment yet you are not necessarily less embarrassed just because it's not your fault. I can be embarrassed when someone I am with forgets the name of the person to be introduced; I can be embarrassed when it is someone else's zip that is undone. It is difficult to think of an equivalent to this in shyness and we don't say that we feel shy for someone else. Other people's shyness can make you shy but generally the shy person is preoccupied with their own behaviour in the situation.

HOW DID YOU FEEL AT THE TIME?

You probably were 'thrown' by the incident. You feel awkward and ill at ease. Often you feel foolish and your embarrassment finds expression in an involuntary and sheepish smile. Feelings of intense self-consciousness also accompany embarrassment. You believe yourself to be the focus of attention. Sometimes people say they wish the ground would open up and swallow them. The self-consciousness that you feel is very similar to the experience of shyness. You feel as if you are a spectator of your behaviour, and this makes it very difficult to behave in a natural way and not be inhibited. It can be very unpleasant to experience this state of mind.

WHAT GESTURES AND EXPRESSIONS ACCOMPANIED YOUR EMBARRASSMENT?

Embarrassment is accompanied by a distinctive emotional display, involving a pattern of looking away from others, making involuntary head movements, touching or covering the face, smiling, blushing, and adopting a stiff posture. Again, many of these are typical of the signs of shyness. The shy person looks down and away, avoids making eye contact, touches the face, and often blushes.

## WHAT BEHAVIOURS ACCOMPANIED YOUR EMBARRASSMENT?

Embarrassment can result in silence as you are at a loss for words, uncertain what to say to put matters right. It is often accompanied by an inability to act, where you are 'frozen'.

The opposite of embarrassment is poise: feeling self-assured and confident, aware of what to say or do in a social situation. Of course, self-assurance and confidence are the very qualities that the shy are convinced that they lack. Embarrassment is what you fear when you are a shy person. Unfortunately, when you are shy you might be more likely than other people to feel embarrassed. Your quietness and feelings of awkwardness might create a predicament in your own mind even if this is not picked up by others present. There is always the fear that it will be picked up. If you are always monitoring your own behaviour, constantly wondering if you are behaving correctly or saying the right thing this experience inevitably becomes close to embarrassment.

Imagine going to a 'posh' restaurant or dinner party with people that you do not know very well or with your managers from work. It quickly becomes clear that there are rules or conventions about which cutlery to use, how particular foods are to be eaten, which glass to use for which drink, and so on. If this is all new to you, you can become hesitant, watch others and try to take your cue from what they do. You don't initiate an action until you have evidence that it is a correct one. In short, you behave in a shy, inhibited way, quite unlike the way you behave when eating with friends or in a familiar environment. What is it that constrains you? You are not likely to poison yourself or become ill. What constrains you is embarrassment, the fear that you will show yourself up and that others will think badly of you.

## WHAT, IF ANYTHING, DID YOU DO TO COPE WITH YOUR EMBARRASSMENT?

One approach to coping is to do nothing – to hope that no one has noticed or that the predicament will just go away.

Sometimes this works and you might be able to cover up a mistake before anyone does notice. Sometimes it is everyone's best interests that those who have witnessed your mistake or loss of poise pretend that they haven't noticed. This helps you to regain your poise and carry on with what you were doing. Why should people help you out in this way? One answer is that your embarrassment creates problems for them too. They won't be able to get things moving again either. The cause of the embarrassment 'hangs in the air' making it difficult for the conversation or meeting to resume. So the waiter may pretend not to notice that you have picked up the wrong cutlery; the visiting speaker will not seem to notice that you mispronounced his name. The doctor or nurse may notice your embarrassment when you describe your worries but give you the impression that they are interpreting these signs as the normal anxiety anyone feels in an unfamiliar situation.

Another form of coping is to make an apology. If you apologize for your behaviour you are showing others that you recognize that the expectations for acceptable behaviour have been infringed. You show too that you acknowledge that these expectations are important. You also show that you accept responsibility for what you have done wrong. An apology can be very effective if it is sincerely given or if it is convincing. If you fail to apologize you run the risk of being seen as boorish, rude, unpleasant or immodest. An apology helps you to be seen as a worthy person who has simply got something wrong. It helps others too as it shows them a way to deal with the predicament that you have created, whether or not this was deliberate. They can accept your apology. They can minimize the significance of your mistake because you have apologized. They can show sympathy to you.

Alternatively you can offer an excuse or a justification for your conduct. When you make an excuse you admit that you have done something wrong but you disclaim responsibility for it: 'I did not let you know I was going to be late because I couldn't get a signal on my phone.' In offering a justification you do accept responsibility but try to minimize the effects of your action: 'I didn't let you know I was going to be late but we are still in time for the show.'

Humour can also prove an effective way of managing an awkward situation. Smiling and laughter are frequent reactions of onlookers, and when you are embarrassed you can take advantage of the situation's potential for humour to cope with your predicament. There is a close connection between humour and embarrassment. Stories about predicaments often induce a smile and embarrassing situations are a regular source of humour. Slipping on a banana skin is a definitive embarrassing event and is at the heart of slapstick comedy. Pride comes before a fall but embarrassment and laughter soon follow it. Often the goal of teasing and coining humorous nicknames for someone is to create embarrassment in the victim; blushing and other signs can be a signal that the tease has been effective. If you are shy or sensitive you can find it very difficult to join in teasing and joking. Humour also provides a means of recovering from embarrassment: if someone present can make a joke about it or 'laugh it off' this provides everyone present with a way to break the deadlock so that they can get the social encounter up and running again.

## THE GOOD AND BAD SIDES OF EMBARRASSMENT

Despite its connection with humour, embarrassment is a serious matter. It can be an intensely painful experience and people will go to enormous lengths to avoid it.

- We may put off seeking medical advice about particular symptoms because of the embarrassment of explaining them to the doctor or of being examined by the doctor. We put it off even though we are worried about the symptoms and we are aware that if they are indications of the existence of a condition, the condition may get worse the longer that diagnosis is postponed. Testicular cancer or prostrate problems are conditions where many men are reluctant to see their doctor and put themselves at risk by putting off an examination.

- We may be reluctant to give or to receive sex education.
  Parents and teachers can be too embarrassed to bring up the topic and children can be too embarrassed to hear the topic raised. The embarrassment of purchasing condoms has long been a staple of comedy. Yet large numbers of sexually transmitted diseases and unwanted pregnancies could be avoided if there were less shyness and embarrassment about these topics.

- We may avoid taking physical exercise because of embarrassment about our bodies.
  There is growing concern about obesity and its related health risks. Many of us are reluctant to go jogging or swimming because of self-consciousness about our body. Many children stop participating in physical exercise at school because they are embarrassed about their appearance particularly in the presence of the opposite sex. Surveys suggest, for example, that forty per cent of girls give up sport by the time they reach their teens and that half of fifteen-year-old girls are not meeting the recommended daily level of exercise. Low self-esteem about body shape is one source of embarrassment. Another source frequently mentioned in surveys is difficulty in maintaining modesty while wearing PE outfits in games lessons. Taking steps to reduce embarrassment is considered to be a key element in increasing the participation of girls and boys in physical exercise.

In summary, fear of embarrassment exerts a powerful influence on us all. It may be one of the factors that sustains shyness and social anxiety. In chapters 5 and 10 we consider the place of fear of embarrassment in the definition of social phobia and social anxiety disorder.

Finally, it is important to emphasize that despite the pain that embarrassment can cause, it can be very useful. It facilitates the smooth running of everyday life. It provides a means for stopping and restarting a social encounter before any problems that have arisen lead to a complete breakdown or become too serious for future interactions to take place. Better that there is embarrassment than that there is anger or rejection. Displaying embarrassment does diffuse anger and shows that the individual is sorry for the predicament and any offence that may have been caused. The punishment it provides for behaviour that breaks a rule – the unpleasant feelings of embarrassment – is severe enough to restrain behaviour but not so severe that it prevents us from future involvement with the other people present.

## Fearfulness, timidity, wariness

These adjectives get us close to the meaning of the word shyness that is emphasized in this book. In its definition of shyness, the Oxford English Dictionary refers to fear, timidity, caution, and aversion. In this sense shyness is not specific to humans but to other animals as well; for example, horses are said to shy from things that are unexpected or that they fear. They pull back, try to move away. At a particular stage in their development most young children show shyness when a stranger approaches. They hide behind mother or refuse to look at the stranger, perhaps covering the face with their hands. Adults are also wary of the unexpected or the threatening, and the word shyness is often used to describe this wariness when we are apprehensive about being the centre of attention; we have heard commentators in the media label someone who is reluctant to take part in their programme or article as 'camera shy', 'interview shy', or 'press shy'. These expressions too, convey the notion of avoidance, of trying to distance yourself from the feared situation.

Shyness and timidity are intimately connected, for example, *timidité* is the French word for shyness. Timidity is close to nervousness and fearfulness, and much of psychological research and clinical treatment of social difficulties has identified shyness with anxiety, as the general term that we have been using – 'social anxiety' – indicates. Research into the antecedents of shyness in infant and childhood temperament connects inhibition with activity of the brain and nervous system involved in fear responses. We discuss this further in chapter 4 when we consider the possible temperamental basis of shyness.

When people talk about their shyness they don't necessarily talk of nervousness or anxiety. Yet the thoughts, feelings and bodily sensations that they describe are often those that accompany fear – sweating, butterflies in the stomach, and so on, which reinforces the view of psychologists and psychiatrists that this is an anxiety condition. This has become such established usage that it is scarcely examined. Nevertheless, we should be hesitant to equate shyness and timidity. Shyness is specific to social situations – Charles Darwin provided the example of a man who is fearless in battle but is shy with strangers. Also, as we explore elsewhere in this book, shyness involves an element of conflict. This can be seen in the shy child who hides when the stranger arrives but who cannot resist looking out from behind his mother or who peeps at the stranger between his fingers. The child might make tentative attempts at approach. A slightly older child may 'hover' beside a game that other children are playing, wanting to join in but hesitant to take the step that is needed to do so. An adolescent may find someone attractive but lack the confidence to take this further. This pattern anticipates the behaviour of the shy adult who wants to interact with others but who lacks self-confidence in the ability to do so. There is threat in the social situation but there is also reward. This conflict is a source of tension, but it is also an incentive for the shy person to overcome his or her anxieties. We return to this issue in chapter 4.

So far we have reflected on uses of shyness in everyday language. It is not a word with a single meaning that can be defined in a short phrase. It has several connotations, and shares features with other concepts. It is hesitancy, an interruption of ongoing activity. It is holding back, reluctance to engage. It is self-consciousness, with a heightened awareness of the self in the social situation. It is not the natural state of affairs. In chapter 4 we examine shyness more closely and describe findings from research that asks large numbers of people about their experience of shyness. We invite you to compare these with your experiences.

## Key points

- Shyness is frequently identified with quietness, nevertheless many apparently outgoing people think of themselves as shy. Often 'scripted' social situations and performances which make roles available provide an outlet for shy people to overcome their inhibition.
- Quietness becomes shyness when the person wants to contribute but is inhibited from doing so. Silence and passive behaviour are accompanied by intense mental activity and rehearsal of possible things to say.
- The concept of shyness overlaps with modesty; they share reserve and diffidence. Modesty is more likely than shyness to be viewed in a positive light.
- Other societies do not necessarily share the negative view that is taken of shyness in most Western societies. Shyness, reserve, and quietness can be viewed as a positive quality in some societies and this leads us to reflect on why our society considers it to be a sign of immaturity or lack of confidence.

- Shyness also overlaps with embarrassment; in particular they share feelings of self-consciousness and awkwardness. Embarrassment seems to be elicited by specific events whereas shyness seems to be about the anticipation of things going wrong.
- Embarrassment is an unpleasant state. Yet it fulfils valuable social functions and contributes to the smooth running of society.
- The fear of embarrassment exerts a powerful influence on behaviour. It can lead to serious problems if it leads to avoidance of medical help or tackling important issues. Fear of embarrassment is a factor in social anxiety.
- Shyness shares features with timidity although it is specific to social situations; one can be shy yet have no timidity in sport or other activities.

# 4

# The experience of shyness

We begin this chapter by inviting you to reflect on your own experience of shyness. You may find it valuable to compare your experience with the descriptions of shyness that other people have provided and the interpretations of these that we offer. We believe that the exercise will be more effective if you write down your answers to the questions that we ask you about your shyness before you continue to read the chapter. Of course there's no obligation to do so if you prefer not to!

## Feeling shy

Think of a recent specific situation where you felt shy. Visualize this as clearly as you can and, keeping it in mind, write answers to the following questions:

1. Briefly describe the situation: when and where it took place, the people who were present, what their relation was to you. Imagine that you are the scriptwriter or director of a television drama, setting the scene for your actors.

2. Did your shyness take an overt form – visible to others present – for example in the way that you spoke? Or in your posture? Were there any visible changes like blushing or sweating?

3. Would others who were present have thought you were shy, or do you think they wouldn't have noticed?

4. What thoughts were going through your mind while you were in this situation? Try to recall as many of these thoughts as you can.

5. Did you think about yourself a lot while you were in the situation? Did you reflect on yourself feeling shy, being too quiet or being a shy person?

6. What bodily feelings or sensations were you aware of?

The next question is perhaps less straightforward to answer:

7. Sometimes we are engrossed in something that absorbs our attention and we are not conscious of ourselves or of anyone else. At other times we have an impression that we are looking at things outside ourselves, something or someone else is the object of our attention and we are a kind of spectator. At yet other times we seem to be observing ourselves in the situation as if we were seeing it from someone else's point of view. Looking back at the situation that you have in mind, which of these perspectives best describes your experience of shyness?
   • I was engrossed in what was going on.
   • I was more conscious of other people than I was of myself.
   • I was more conscious of myself than I was of anyone else.

*1. Briefly describe the situation: when and where it took place, the people who were present, what their relation was to you. Imagine that you are the scriptwriter or director of a television drama, setting the scene for your actors.*

What situation did you describe? It is difficult for us to predict what you chose to describe because a variety of situations elicit shyness. However, there are some kinds of situations that are more likely to make most of us feel shy:

- One kind that is frequently mentioned is when you are in a large group, particularly when you are – or believe you are – the focus of others' attention. Making a presentation at work or college is one common example. Having to give a speech at a wedding or a dinner is challenging even for people who interact a lot with others in their daily life.
- When you are interacting with strangers, meeting someone for the first time, being introduced to someone, or entering a situation where you don't know many people or where you are unfamiliar with how to behave.
- Small social events such as parties or dinners when you have to make conversation with others.
- Being the focus of attention when, for example, someone asks you for your opinion and you have to speak up in front of others.
- Being evaluated by others, for example during an interview or a viva examination.
- When you interact with someone of the opposite sex or if you enter a place that is reserved for or largely occupied by the other sex such as being the only woman in a group of men or the only man in a group of women.
- Asking someone for a date or meeting someone on the first date.
- When you have to be assertive, to stand up for your rights as when complaining about poor service or pointing out someone's mistake.
- When you have to ask someone for help or for a favour.
- Speaking to an authority figure such as your manager at work, your teacher, a doctor, a minister of religion or a bank manager.

- Speaking to someone who is an expert in a field that you are expected to know something about or about which you are supposed to be an expert.
- Dealing with being criticized or being involved in arguments, conflicts, and disagreements.
- Speaking to someone in an informal setting even though you are familiar with him or her in a work setting. For example, you might be confident in interacting with colleagues at work but be shy with them outside work or when conversing about non-work topics.
- The presence of specific types of people can induce shyness, for example being shy when interacting with older people or with children. Some people report being shy even with their parents, their children or other relatives.

The experience described in Case 1 is not unusual. There is a vivid account of a similar experience in the novel *Adolphe* by the nineteenth-century French writer, Benjamin Constant, which describes how Adolphe's father was always overcome with shyness in his son's company. His inhibition prevented him from expressing any affection for his son and this came across as

Case 1

I was always shy when I was alone with my father because I could never think of anything to say to him. He was quite difficult to talk to and he never had much to say to me. I think this was partly to do with his shyness and partly because we had few interests in common. There would always be long silences which made me very uncomfortable. I would feel more relaxed when he left or when someone else arrived to join in the conversation. This person often would interrupt a silence and begin a conversation. I would feel guilty about feeling this way, about talking to them and not to him. I also felt guilty when I was chatting with someone and he arrived and I would just clam up.

coldness. This discouraged any signs of affection from Adolphe in return, which led his father to believe that his son did not love him. On the other hand, while he was unable to show any affection in his son's presence he was able to express his feelings in letters to him and these letters were warm and friendly. It was only later that Adolphe became aware that shyness was the reason for his father's apparent coldness and of course he came to think of his father quite differently when he realized this.

Can we detect any common threads in this variety of situations? Two features seem to characterize these situations. One is their unfamiliarity; the other is fear of being evaluated.

- We are more likely to be shy when meeting strangers or when encountering situations which are novel or with which we are unfamiliar. This seems fundamental to one sense of the word shyness and is a reaction that resembles fear of the unknown. It is very widespread and many people who are initially shy overcome this when they become more familiar with the other people involved or with the demands of the situation. New students who have left home for university, for example, are often shy at first but become less so over time. Starting a new job or moving house can induce shyness until we get to know our new colleagues or neighbours.
- Being evaluated by others is common to many of the situations that are frequently mentioned and underlies anxieties about speaking up in front of other people even though we know them. These anxieties do not necessarily decrease with increasing familiarity and they reflect our ongoing apprehension about what other people will think of us. There are different concerns in this. One is the low self-esteem we have about some aspect of our self. A student is shy in class discussion because she fears that she will expose her ignorance or lack of sophistication to others. She may say something

that others will think stupid or will repeat a point that has already been made. Her shyness is a form of hiding. Even when she does contribute something that receives a positive reception from others she will not necessarily gain confidence from this. Either she was fortunate on this occasion or she has further to fall if she does say something foolish in the future. Better to quit when you are ahead! A second reason for shyness is that you will reveal your shyness or lack of social competence to others. This is also a lack of self-confidence but it is low self-esteem about you as a social actor. Again, your strategy might be to remain quiet and keep in the background, as you are less likely to demonstrate your lack of social skills.

Shy people can find it difficult to be assertive when standing up for their rights. One of the problems they face is that these situations have the potential to become difficult, to involve conflict with others. Managing conflict can require qualities of poise and the exercise of good judgement and these can be difficult to attain when you are anxious and self-conscious. The lowered eyes and reluctance to make eye contact typical of shyness resemble a display of submission and this, together with hesitance to contribute to interaction, can constrain the social roles that are open to shy individuals. Shy people also often adopt a 'nice' persona. They tend to be ingratiating, to agree with others and to keep their own opinions to themselves if these are different from those of others present. This is essentially a form of social withdrawal – keeping in the background and not drawing attention to yourself. It means that you do not have to face the challenges of sustaining arguments or standing up for yourself. Niceness can be a positive attribute of shyness and make the shy person pleasant and likeable but it has limitations, especially when the circumstances require you to be assertive: you may lack the skills to do so and the change in your persona might appear aggressive to others rather than assertive. This pattern has been labelled 'chronic niceness'.

*2. Did your shyness take an overt form – visible to others present – for example in the way that you spoke? Or in your posture? Were there any visible changes like blushing or sweating?*

For many people shyness takes the form of silence, a reluctance to contribute to conversation that seems to be due to inhibition: you want to do so but you just can't. You are aware that you are the silent person in the room or in the meeting or conversation. When you do speak, for example if you are asked a question or if you pluck up the courage to say something, you do so with a very quiet voice and you feel inhibited about raising your voice. Often too your voice is flat without variety of pitch or emphasis. You become very conscious of your voice, as if you are an objective listener to what you are saying. You may also stammer or stutter. You tend not to look directly at other people and do not make eye contact with them. You may nod and smile a lot to show that you are following the conversation even though you are not contributing yourself. This also helps to maintain some contact with the group so that you do not become separated from it even though you are not an active participant. Your posture and gestures can also reveal inhibition and self-consciousness: they can be stiff and awkward.

Blushing, sweating, and trembling can also accompany shyness – blushing is very commonly mentioned as a symptom of shyness – and these symptoms can be visible to others. We shall see in our discussion of social anxiety disorder in later chapters that fear about showing blushing, sweating, and trembling to others is a central element in this disorder. We devote a separate chapter to blushing since it is so frequently mentioned.

These inhibited behaviours are, or at least can be, noticed by others and this is a concern of shy people. They lack confidence in their ability to behave effectively in company. However, there is more to shyness than reticence. Some people feel shy without demonstrating any overt signs of it. They can be confident in the impression that they create in others. But inside it is a different matter. They share the feelings of anxiety that the demonstrably shy person does. We discuss these feelings later in this section. We are often surprised to learn of celebrities or people in the public eye that underneath their apparently confident appearance they are shy. Yet the confident impression they convey is not achieved easily or without cost and they rarely feel at ease in these situations.

*3. Would others who were present have thought you were shy, or do you think they wouldn't have noticed?*

As we have seen many shy people are preoccupied with what others present might think of them and this preoccupation can influence their perception of the situation. You can easily exaggerate in your mind the degree of attention that others pay to you or how much of your behaviour others notice. Others might not notice that you are being quiet. Even if they do so, they might not attribute this to shyness. They might see it as natural quietness since we all know that not everyone is noisy or extraverted. This preoccupation with what others think is also central to social anxiety disorder and we shall see that psychological interventions to help people with this disorder concentrate on the misperceptions that anxious people have and the inferences that they make about what others must think of them.

*4. What thoughts were going through your mind while you were in this situation?*
*5. Did you think about yourself a lot while you were in the situation? Did you reflect on yourself feeling shy, being too quiet or being a shy person?*

We consider these two questions together. Shy people emphasize that the outwardly passive behaviour that frequently represents their shyness is accompanied by intense mental activity. In particular shy people are self-conscious, that is, they are very aware of themselves in the situation. We discuss this below. The shy person also thinks about how unpleasant the situation is: he or she wishes that the situation would come to an end so that they could be elsewhere. When you are shy you are preoccupied with yourself but at the same time you are constantly monitoring the situation, thinking whether you should speak, rehearsing things you might say, trying to gauge what you could say without appearing foolish or giving yourself away. At the same time you are thinking about your inadequacy, feeling stupid or out of place, not belonging. You are also wondering what other people who are present think of you and what kind of impression you are creating. It is hard not to think about your shyness, to believe that your difficulties are due to this. It is exhausting just to think of the things that go through the shy person's mind and shy people do find social situations exhausting.

### 6. What bodily feelings or sensations were you aware of?

The physiological symptoms that accompany shyness are similar to those that are involved in the 'fight or flight' reactions typical of fear: heart pounding, increased pulse, dry mouth, perspiration, and butterflies in the stomach. As is well known, these reactions are essential for mobilizing the resources of the body in order to take effective action in the face of threat and they are found in both humans and animals. They have evolved to enable us to react quickly to physical danger. One consequence of their evolved nature is that they are difficult to control and early signs of danger can trigger the pattern of reactions before we have conscious awareness of the threat. So even if I tell myself before going into the interview room or before speaking up in front of a room full of people that I am going to be calm and I remind myself that I have successfully undertaken these or similar activities many times before, this is not enough in itself to head off anxious symptoms, which seem to arise, unwanted, by themselves. An additional problem, and one that is frequently mentioned by shy people, is that anxious feelings make it difficult for them to think clearly in the presence of the threat and this, in turn, interferes with selecting appropriate behaviour which results in further increases in anxiety. Yet another problem is that I imagine that my symptoms of anxiety will be visible to others and I believe that they will think badly of me because of this. Not surprisingly, feelings of anxiety about – and in – social situations is fundamental to many people's shyness and social anxiety and finding ways of dealing with this has a central place in this book.

*7. Looking back at the situation that you have in mind, which of these perspectives best describes your experience of shyness?*
- *I was engrossed in what was going on.*
- *I was more conscious of other people than I was of myself.*
- *I was more conscious of myself than I was of anyone else.*

Self-consciousness is fundamental to the experience of shyness. When we are self-conscious we are not engrossed in what is going on. Our attention is focused on our self. This has a number of unfortunate consequences:

- We become more aware of our bodily states. This increased awareness can make us more anxious as we become aware that we are anxious and this magnifies our anxiety. Similarly, awareness that you are blushing intensifies your blush.
- We find it hard to fit in with the conversation; our thoughts are preoccupied with ourselves and not with the topic of conversation.
- We miss the subtle signals that other people give about taking turns in conversation and we don't give any appropriate signals ourselves. It becomes difficult to judge just when to make a contribution and what to contribute.

- We become preoccupied with how we appear to others but we do not pay enough attention to others to determine what kind of impression we are actually making.
- We tend to focus on negative aspects of our self. Research has shown this is likely to happen even if we weren't initially feeling negative about our self.

The Stanford Shyness Survey identified self-consciousness as the most frequently endorsed of all the symptoms of shyness (reported by eighty-five per cent of participants in the survey). Self-consciousness is an inherently unpleasant state where you see yourself as if from the outside and where you feel out of place and your actions seem forced and unnatural. This experience is dominated by our sense of how we appear in the eyes of others. This implies that the less self-confident we are the more self-conscious we will be. Self-consciousness is an unpleasant state of mind and it can make it very difficult to act naturally or spontaneously. Often our outwardly silent and passive behaviour is accompanied by this intense mental activity where we are constantly judging ourselves. We shall see that self-consciousness – or self-focused attention as psychologists sometimes label it – is experienced in social anxiety disorder and cognitive approaches to treating this disorder try to shift the focus of attention away from the self.

When you are not shy you can become engrossed in the topic of conversation and pay more attention to it. Because you are not preoccupied with yourself and the impression you are making you have more mental resources to devote to thinking about the topic, to planning ahead or getting your thoughts in order. You rehearse less and can time your contributions more appropriately. In short, self-conscious thoughts interfere with your involvement. One of the goals of interventions to help shy people is to reduce their self-consciousness.

## Box 1: Self-consciousness

Some psychologists describe this experience in terms of a duality where we have the sense of being observed from another perspective or as if we are observed by an 'other'. They emphasize the perspective that we imagine the other takes on us and on our behaviour. This is a very old idea in philosophy and psychology. The philosopher Adam Smith described it in 1759:

> When I endeavour to examine my own conduct ... I divide myself into two characters, as it were into two persons; and that I, the examiner and judge, represent a different character from that other I, the person whose conduct is examined into and judged of. The first is spectator, whose sentiments with regard to my own conduct I endeavour to enter into, by placing myself in his situation, and by considering how it would appear to me, when seen from that particular point of view.

Smith characterizes the other's viewpoint as that of a neutral observer. The psychologist Helen Block Lewis conceives of the imagined observer taking a less neutral perspective: she writes about the 'implied hostile watcher'. As we see in chapter 7, learning to observe yourself is an important component in cognitive behaviour therapy (CBT). The emphasis in CBT is on learning how to take an objective perspective and not being judgemental. Also, the perspective you are taking is your own, not that of an imagined watcher or audience.

## An experiment

One approach to doing so is by means of the behavioural experiments that we outline in later chapters. For example, you can deliberately try to focus your attention on another person or on other people with whom you are interacting. Pay close attention to them for a pre-set period of time of a few minutes. How do they look? What are they wearing? What might they be thinking? What facial expressions do they adopt? Are they speaking or listening? What are they saying? Try to notice and remember as much as you can so that you have a detailed record of this. Make a note too of how *you* feel during this period. Practise this so that you become good at noticing. You might compare your experience with how you normally feel. But you could extend this behavioural experiment. Instead of focusing attention on the other you could deliberately focus attention on yourself. What feelings are you aware of? What facial expressions are you adopting? Again, practise this.

Experiments like this can increase your sensitivity to others. They can demonstrate to you the difference between self-focused and other-focused attention. They show you how much information you are missing when you are self-focused. They can demonstrate how less anxious you feel when you do not focus on yourself.

It is important that you undertake experiments like these rather than just think about them. It is important too to approach them systematically, planning and implementing them and keeping a record of your feelings and your findings. Doing it now and then or in a haphazard fashion won't help. You might find it easier to introduce them during meetings with people you know before attempting it with people or in situations that typically make you shy.

## Being a shy person

Do you consider yourself to be a shy person? We have described findings from the Stanford Shyness Survey that a high proportion of people across the world describe themselves as shy people. Shyness is not an infrequent experience for them but is part of their personality. In many cases it is part of their personality that they are unhappy with. Many psychologists consider shyness to be a personality trait: some people are shy and others are less so. Traits can be measured in different ways, including by self-report questionnaires. Box 2 presents an example of a measure of shyness, and you might like to complete this now.

## Box 2: How shy are you?

*Take the Shyness Quiz to find out*

For each of the seven questions below tick the answer (1, 2, or 3) which best describes you.

1.  How often do you experience feelings of shyness?
    1.  Once a month or less
    2.  Nearly every other day
    3.  Constantly, several times a day

2.  Compared with your peers, how shy are you?
    1.  Much less shy
    2.  About as shy
    3.  Much more shy

3.  'Shyness makes me feel symptoms such as a racing heart and sweaty palms.' This description is:
    1.  Not like me
    2.  Somewhat like me
    3.  A lot like me

4.  'Shyness makes me think others are reacting negatively to what I do and say.' This description is:
    1.  Not like me
    2.  Somewhat like me
    3.  A lot like me

5.  'Shyness keeps me from behaving appropriately in social settings – for example, introducing myself or making conversation.' This description is:
    1.  Not like me
    2.  Somewhat like me
    3.  A lot like me

6.  'Shyness appears when I'm interacting with someone to whom I'm attracted.' This description is:
    1.  Not like me
    2.  Somewhat like me
    3.  A lot like me

*Continued*

7. 'Shyness appears when I'm interacting with someone in a position of authority' (such as supervisors at work, professors, experts in their field). This description is:
   1. Not like me
   2. Somewhat like me
   3. A lot like me

**Scoring the Shyness Quiz:** Add together the numbers that correspond to your responses to each of the seven items in the Shyness Quiz. For example, if you answered 2 to Question 1 and 3 to Question 2, you would add 2 + 3. Continue until you have added all seven numbers.

**7–11:** Not at all to slightly shy: Shyness does not seem to be much of a problem for you.

**12–16:** Moderately shy: Shyness seems to be a frequent barrier in your life.

**17–21:** Very shy: Shyness is preventing you from reaching your full potential in life.

Reproduced by permission of Professor Bernardo J. Carducci, The Shyness Research Institute at Indiana University Southeast, USA

How do shy people differ from those who are less shy? You might expect that people who do not consider themselves to be shy or who obtain low scores on a measure of shyness would answer the questions we have been presenting in quite different ways from shy people. But this turns out not to be the case. Everyone tends to agree on what kinds of situations are most challenging and how they react when they do feel shy. Shy people express more anxiety about these situations and this may be because they explain the difficulties they experience in terms of their own personality and not in terms of the demands that these situations make on anyone.

## Shyness as a personality trait

Is there something that makes people shy in the first place? Is being shy a matter of your personality? Are you born shy or is shyness something that you acquire; for example to do with your relationships with your parents or how you were brought up? And if it is part of your personality, can it be changed? And if it can't, how can you overcome your shyness? We won't dwell on shyness as a trait or on the causes of shyness in this book as the techniques for coping with shyness and social anxiety aren't dependent on personality. Unlike other approaches to psychotherapy they don't explore the individual's life history or seek explanations in the past. They concentrate on the present and the future and aim to bring about change, whatever the personality of the person who is aiming to change.

There is evidence of shyness-related behaviour in very young children and this is of interest in itself. As we shall see, the evidence does not conclude that a shy personality is fixed at an early age. Some influential psychological research into infancy and childhood has concluded that individual differences in temperament appear early in life that predispose an individual to be shy. One of the leaders of this research has been the American developmental psychologist Jerome Kagan who has studied young children, following their development from infancy into adolescence. His studies, as well as research conducted by many other psychologists, suggest that the origins of shyness may lie in a child's temperament, which Kagan has labelled 'behavioral inhibition to the unfamiliar'. Evidence from this research shows that:

- Some infants at four months show a pattern of 'emotional reactivity' – crying, thrashing movements of arms and legs, and arching the back when encountering a novel situation. Other children are much calmer in the same circumstances.
- These highly reactive infants are more likely to become inhibited from the second year onwards. When they encounter novel events and unfamiliar people they react

by fretting, crying, making distress calls, and trying to withdraw. They make no spontaneous approaches to an unfamiliar adult they are meeting.

- As inhibited children grow older their reactions to unfamiliarity are characterized by quietness, seldom smiling and withdrawal and they tend to be described by their mothers and teachers as shy children. On the other hand, the uninhibited children are quick to adapt, are sociable and friendly with others who are present.
- Inhibited and uninhibited children differ on physiological measures related to fight or flight reactions. These include measures of heart rate and secretion of adrenalin and cortisol. When adrenalin is released into the bloodstream, it brings about increases in heart rate, raises sugar levels in the blood, dilates the pupils and redirects blood to the musculature and away from the skin and gut. Cortisol is a hormone that is also secreted into the bloodstream to release protein to provide extra energy. Reactions to stress also include changes to the musculature involved in vocal production, producing an increase in the voice fundamental frequency and reduction in its variability and increase in rate of articulation. These changes can readily be detected as flatness of tone, high-pitched voice and increased rate of speaking.
- In addition to the reactivity of the autonomic nervous system there are other biologically based differences between inhibited and uninhibited children. More children with blue eyes are found in samples of inhibited children than would be expected on the basis of the distribution of blue eyes in the population. Shy children tend to have narrower faces than do non-shy children. They are more susceptible to allergies and to be absent from school with minor ailments.

Does all this mean that we are born shy? The short answer is No.

First, consistently inhibited children who remain shy from one age to another comprise only a small minority – some ten per cent – of the children who have been studied. On the other hand, much more than ten per cent of the population consider themselves to be shy, implying that there are many shy older children and adults who were not necessarily shy at an early age. Some children who were initially shy become less so over time; some who were not shy at that age become shy later.

This research starts with infants who are reactive or inhibited; it does not start with shy older children or adults to look back at their early years to see if they were reactive or inhibited in early life.

Third, the physiological pattern that defines inhibition is related to fear: it is the system that is involved in fight and flight. Shyness might not be simply fear, even if many shy people do express anxiety about social situations: anxiety might be a consequence of their shyness rather than intrinsic to its nature.

Fourth, inhibition is defined in terms of unfamiliar events of all kinds whereas shyness seems to be a specific reaction to other people; in addition, as we have seen, people are also shy with familiar people and in familiar settings including work, school and even in their own families.

Future research will throw light on the connection between temperament and shyness and will discover more about the origins of shyness.

There are other factors that influence the development of shyness. It may have a genetic basis where parents pass their genes for shyness to their child. Parental genes can also influence the child's shyness if their shy behaviour serves as a model for the child's behaviour in the presence of others or if they adopt a socially withdrawn lifestyle that limits the child's opportunities for learning how to interact effectively with others. Research shows that parents may also influence their child's development if they are overprotective of their child's shyness. This also limits the child's opportunities for learning how to interact and may heighten the child's anxiety by drawing attention to the difficulties or dangers of social interaction.

We conclude consideration of shyness as a trait by discussing some of the consequences for shy people of their shyness.

## Some unwanted consequences of shyness

Shy people describe many unwanted consequences of their shyness. One is that they feel they are often misjudged by others and are seen as cold, aloof, unfriendly, having no interest in anyone else, conceited, and even rude. This is because their inhibition unintentionally produces behaviour that is often inappropriate to the setting and breaks unwritten rules about social interactions.

- If someone says hello to you, it is expected that you should respond in similar fashion.
- If you enter a room that someone is in you should acknowledge their presence in some way, perhaps by greeting them or smiling at them.
- If someone does something for you then thanks are expected, and so on.

Shy people can fail to make the appropriate responses in these circumstances and may be seen as rude or unfriendly. Shy persons can fail to respond not because they do not know what they are supposed to do or how to do it, but because their shyness inhibits them from doing what is needed. If the other person does not realize that this lack of response is due to shyness then the behaviour will appear rude or odd in some way.

Shy people also report that their good qualities often go unnoticed and that they are passed over when individuals are

### Case 2

> I was a prefect at school and arrived early to be at the doors to see that everyone arrived on time. I would pass the same teacher every morning in the empty corridor and he would say 'good morning' but I was so shy that I would look away from him before our paths crossed, I would blush and not say anything. One day in class he complained about the rudeness of pupils and without naming me gave my failure to acknowledge him in the corridor as an example of rudeness.

selected for teams or membership of groups, or are put forward for promotion or positions of responsibility. Again, this can be an unintended consequence of the shy person's demeanour or tendency to remain quiet and keep in the background. This can be due to the inhibition that is often experienced when encountering authority figures, as in the prefect's awkward encounters in the corridor with his teacher.

Shy people can find it difficult to establish romantic relationships, to ask for dates or to behave effectively when on a date. These are situations where it is important for the individual to make a good impression on the other, to appear attractive to the other. They are not situations where the shy person can hide and this can create unpleasant feelings of self-consciousness. These situations often involve the person adopting an unfamiliar role; most of us are familiar with the role at least at second hand, from movies, television programmes and books. Putting this knowledge into practice is hard when you lack confidence in yourself and self-consciousness interferes with your thinking. A study that followed shy children into adulthood found that shy men took longer than non-shy men to form romantic attachments and to get married. There was no similar trend for the shy girls in the study as shy women were no slower to reach these milestones than non-shy women were. The researchers interpreted this gender difference in terms of cultural expectations at the time when the children were growing up, as men were expected to take the initiative in contacting women. Being a shy, modest or reserved woman might have been no disadvantage as these could be viewed as positive qualities. However, they would make it more difficult for shy men to play the role expected of them.

## Overcoming shyness

Can shyness be overcome? The short answer is Yes. Whether or not shyness is an aspect of your personality is not the issue if you wish to change. We are not talking about changing your personality but about changing specific targeted beliefs and behaviours. Changes in small things can have a big influence on how we approach the kinds of social situations that have caused us to be anxious. We can feel more comfortable and less anxious without radically altering the person we are. Indeed, we are likely to be more our self, the person whom our friends, and those with whom we are at ease, know

The techniques that we describe in our chapters on social anxiety disorder can be applied to shyness. As we shall see, psychological approaches focus on the beliefs that shy people have about themselves; they focus on reducing self-consciousness; they concentrate on anxiety symptoms and reduce anxiety in a systematic way. All of these approaches involve doing rather than talking or thinking. They involve identifying specific areas of difficulty and working to overcome these. There is no short cut to success yet even brief targeted interventions can be very effective in overcoming shyness. In chapter 5 we discuss the connection between shyness and social anxiety disorder.

## Key points

- A variety of situations can elicit shyness. These range from tasks that would be challenging for most people – giving a speech or making a public presentation – to interactions with familiar others including members of one's own family.
- We can identify two themes in these situations. One is unfamiliarity, whether of people or of setting, where it is not clear how to behave appropriately or one doubts that one has the ability to do so. The second comprises situations where we believe that we are likely to be evaluated and we are not confident that we will be able to make the impression we wish to. Not knowing how to behave or not having the confidence to behave effectively is at the heart of shyness.
- Shyness is associated with being silent, speaking with a quiet voice, staying in the background, and keeping one's opinion to oneself.
- Common symptoms are heart pounding, perspiration, sweating, and butterflies in the stomach, symptoms that are characteristic of anxiety. Blushing also accompanies shyness although this is less obviously an indication of anxiety and more of self-consciousness.
- Self-consciousness is central to shyness. It is an unpleasant state that makes you more aware of your symptoms but give less attention to others, to what they are saying and to the subtle cues that reveal their attitudes to you and which are involved in the management of conversations.
- Self-consciousness can be overcome by practising other-focused attention.
- Shyness is a personality trait that seems to have its beginnings in early childhood. Some very young children demonstrate the behaviours and physiological symptoms typical of shyness. Nevertheless early emotionality does not

necessarily result in later shyness; for some shy people, their shyness is not evident at such an early age.

- Attempts to overcome shyness are not dependent on the individual's history of shyness but concentrate on exercises that are designed to change specific behaviours, notably safety behaviours.

# 5

# What is social anxiety disorder?

## Social anxiety as a clinical condition

Our first chapters have largely concentrated on shyness. We saw that just about everybody has experienced shyness at one time or another, whether this occurs during a particular period in their life or whether it is triggered by particular kinds of situations. We saw too that very many people label themselves as shy and that most of those who do so regard shyness as a problem that they would overcome if they could. In this chapter we examine a clinical approach to helping people overcome the kinds of problems reported by shy and socially anxious people.

Psychiatrists and clinical psychologists developed the concept of social phobia in order to understand these difficulties better and to develop treatments and interventions of various kinds to help people who have social anxieties. The term social anxiety disorder (SAD) is now beginning to replace social phobia. However it is labelled, it represents a medical approach to social difficulties and it is worth thinking about what is entailed by this approach.

We typically seek medical advice because we are concerned about specific symptoms. We describe these symptoms to the doctor who might ask us additional questions about them and perhaps conduct some tests. The doctor has to decide whether these symptoms are indications of a particular illness or medical condition, for example whether other symptoms that the patient hasn't mentioned are also present. The doctor may try to exclude some possible explanations. He or she determines whether a treatment appropriate to the condition can be prescribed, or whether the patient should be referred to a specialist for further tests or for treatment. The doctor has knowledge about a range of conditions, the signs that are indicative of these conditions, and the treatments that are available. Some diagnoses are straightforward. However, in many cases symptoms might be potentially diagnostic of several different conditions and the doctor would have to initiate further investigations to identify the underlying cause of the problem. Before focusing on social anxiety disorder it may be helpful to make some additional brief points here about the nature of diagnosis and treatment.

First, it is easy to think of diagnosis as a mechanical procedure where symptoms clearly point to the condition, but in practice it demands clinical judgement and experience. Symptoms do not necessarily map onto underlying conditions in a straightforward way.

Second, the diagnostic categories that medicine uses – influenza, emphysema, bronchitis, and so on – are not static and impervious to outside influence. Categories are adjusted as more medical knowledge is gained. Distinctions are made among existing conditions and diagnoses are refined. New conditions are identified, AIDS being perhaps the most dramatic. Some conditions increase in prevalence – asthma, autism, and depression are examples of these – and it is not necessarily clear what causes this. Does this change represent an increase in the numbers of people who have the condition? Is it due to changes in diagnosis, either because more people come forward with the symptoms or because diagnosis becomes more exact as more is learned about the condition? Or does the availability of new treatments influence the frequency of diagnosis?

Diagnostic categories change as more and more knowledge is acquired about the causes of conditions. Doctors clearly need to have access to up-to-date information about understanding and treatment of conditions. Research is published in medical journals and published guidelines based on this research are made available to doctors. In psychiatry, information is provided by publications that summarize the major psychiatric disorders and list the symptoms that recent research and clinical practice has established as diagnostic of these conditions. In this book we draw upon the *Diagnostic and Statistical Manual of Mental Disorders*, a handbook for psychiatric diagnoses that is published by the American Psychiatric Association. The manual adopts a categorical system for psychological disorders: if the individual meets a specified set of criteria his or her condition belongs to this particular category; it does not belong to it if not all the criteria are met. The categories of mental disorders are distinct; each one is defined by its own set of criteria. Several editions of this volume have been published – the most recent edition is the fourth edition, text revision, which was published in 2000. The category of social phobia has changed over successive editions of the manual and we discuss this below.

Finally, treatments for particular conditions change, as new therapies and medications are introduced and as clinical research tests the effectiveness of treatments. Treatments for social anxiety disorder include psychological forms of intervention, where cognitive behaviour therapy has become the preferred method of treatment, and pharmaceutical treatments. We discuss these in chapters 7, 8, and 9.

Let us focus now on social anxiety disorder. A patient might approach his or her doctor because they are concerned about their shyness or other difficulties with social situations, for example having panic attacks in public places. A doctor might not regard 'shyness' as a medical condition or diagnostic category even though individuals may seek help because of what they think of as their shyness. They may use this word to label their difficulties, whether these take the form of chronic blushing, excessive anxiety in social situations, failure to find satisfactory romantic relationships, the experience of social isolation, and so on. A doctor would have to decide if the patient is presenting signs of a recognized condition that is amenable to treatment. It is evident that many doctors in the past would not have recognized these signs and this might still be the experience today for many people who seek medical help. Many doctors may fail to diagnose the condition even when the symptoms are clearly presented. Socially anxious people can be incorrectly diagnosed as having panic disorder, depression, or general anxiety. In addition, many socially anxious people hesitate to approach their doctor because of the embarrassment of not being taken seriously or 'wasting the doctor's time' or they are reluctant to describe all their anxieties.

A patient's difficulties in their encounter with their doctor may be due to the doctor's inability to keep up with developments in psychiatry since problems of social anxiety have been recognized as a psychological problem for some time now. The high incidence of these problems in the population is now recognized. Guidelines for diagnosis and for treatment are available. Let us look at these developments.

Psychiatry has developed systems of classification of psychiatric disorders and in this development social phobia emerged as a condition in its own right, appearing in the *Diagnostic and Statistical Manual of Mental Disorders*. In many ways it is an unfortunate label, as we think of a phobia as a short-lived and intense fear of a quite specific target, for example spiders, snakes or the sight of blood. We are however familiar with the use of the word to refer to fear of more diffuse targets, for example, claustrophobia, fear of confined spaces, or agoraphobia (fear of open places – at one time social phobia was grouped along with agoraphobia). The terminology reflects the historical origins of the concept.

The first two editions of the *Diagnostic and Statistical Manual of Mental Disorders* included social fears simply as instances of an undifferentiated category of phobia and it was only in the third edition published in 1980 that social phobia first appeared in its own right. This edition distinguished three kinds of phobias: agoraphobia, simple phobia, and social phobia.

Social phobia was characterized as a persistent fear of situations where the individuals believe they might be subject to scrutiny by others and anticipate that their behaviour will lead to embarrassment or humiliation. This causes them a significant amount of distress because they recognize that the fear is excessive. More recently there has been a shift in terminology, and clinical practitioners are beginning to prefer the term social anxiety disorder. Even this might not do justice to the concerns of the anxious person if it is understood to imply anxiety about social events, a term that might be taken as synonymous with large gatherings or public events. When you are socially anxious in the sense identified by clinical research you are anxious about interacting with other people. These interactions occur anywhere and everywhere, at work, at school, in shops and offices, and even with friends and acquaintances. The socially anxious person is anxious about his or her interactions with other people, particularly those where he or she is the object of attention or has to perform in some way in front of others. Anxious people fear that they will be embarrassed because they will act inappropriately or draw attention to their inadequacies. They fear that they will show signs of anxiety as this too will reveal their inadequacies. This creates a vicious circle, where visible signs of anxieties are cause for further anxiety. All these fears are reflected in the diagnostic criteria for social phobia.

## Avoidant personality disorder

We have seen that the diagnostic category of Social Phobia/Social Anxiety Disorder has been modified over the years. We will see an example of this in the distinction between generalized and specific social phobia which we describe below. The authors of the *Diagnostic and Statistical Manual* introduced a separate condition in the third edition in 1980: avoidant personality disorder. This was defined as a pervasive pattern of social inhibition, feelings of inadequacy, and hypersensitivity to negative evaluation. There has been much discussion since its introduction about the differences between this category and social anxiety disorder and about the relation of each of these to shyness.

As its label makes explicit, this condition is regarded as a form of personality disorder. It involves being detached and having few relationships with other people. As a disorder of personality it may be more ingrained and hence more difficult to change.

One view is that Avoidant Personality Disorder is a more severe form of social anxiety. Perhaps we can think of a scale of social anxiety that ranges from rarely being anxious or occasionally feeling shy at one end of the scale to experiencing intense anxiety at the top of the scale. In this view, shyness would be towards the lower end, generalized social phobia would be higher up the scale, and Avoidant Personality Disorder would be towards the top of the scale. The relations among these levels or forms of anxiety are a topic for ongoing research. This may result in future editions of the manual including more information on the distinctions to be made and their implications for diagnosis and treatment.

Avoidant personality disorder is much less common than social phobia. Studies suggest that the prevalence of avoidant personality disorder in the general population is less than two per cent. Nevertheless, it is common relative to the frequency of diagnosis of other personality disorders, and it constitutes a substantial proportion (twenty–twenty-five per cent) of patients in clinical settings. A survey undertaken in Sweden of a random sample of the population found that sixteen per cent of the population met the criteria for either social anxiety disorder or avoidant personality disorder but the frequency of social anxiety disorder was much greater than that of the latter – seven people met diagnostic criteria for Social Anxiety Disorder for every one person who met the criteria for avoidant personality disorder.

## The diagnosis of social anxiety disorder

It may be helpful here to set out in Box 1 the diagnostic criteria for social anxiety disorder as set out in the *Diagnostic and Statistical Manual of Mental Disorders.*

Box 1: Diagnostic criteria for social phobia

> A.  A marked and persistent fear of one or more social or performance situations involving exposure to unfamiliar people or possible scrutiny by others. The person fears that he or she will act in a way (or show symptoms of anxiety) that will be humiliating or embarrassing. *Note:* In children, there must be evidence of the capacity for age-appropriate social relationships with familiar people and the anxiety must occur in peer settings, not just in interactions with adults.

*Continued*

B. Exposure to the feared social situation almost invariably provokes anxiety, which may take the form of a situationally bound or situationally predisposed panic attack. *Note:* In children, the anxiety may be expressed by crying, tantrums, freezing, or shrinking from social situations with unfamiliar people.

C. The person recognizes that the fear is excessive or unreasonable. *Note:* In children, this feature may be absent.

D. The feared social or performance situations are avoided or endured with intense anxiety or distress.

E. The avoidance, anxious anticipation, or distress in the feared social or performance situation(s) interferes significantly with the person's normal routine, occupational (academic) functioning, or social activities or relationships, or there is marked distress about having the phobia.

F. In individuals under age 18 years, the duration is at least six months.

G. The fear or avoidance is not due to the direct physiological effects of a substance (e.g. a drug of abuse, a medication) or a general medical condition and is not better accounted for by another mental disorder (e.g. panic disorder with or without agoraphobia, separation anxiety disorder, body dysmorphic disorder, a pervasive developmental disorder, or schizoid personality disorder).

H. If a general medical condition or another mental disorder is present, fear in criterion A is unrelated to it, e.g. the fear is not of stuttering, trembling in Parkinson's disease, or exhibiting abnormal eating behavior in Anorexia Nervosa or Bulimia Nervosa.

*Specify if:* **Generalized:** if the fears include most social situations (also consider the additional diagnosis of avoidant personality disorder).

Source: *The Diagnostic and Statistical Manual of Mental Disorders,* fourth edition, Text Revision published by the American Psychiatric Association (2000). Reproduced by permission of the American Psychiatric Association.

All of these criteria have to be met for the diagnosis of social anxiety disorder. The criteria do represent the fears that we discussed above and in the preceding chapters. The situations that are feared tend to be avoided; if you find yourself in one of the feared situations you try to escape. If escape is not possible then you remain in a state of intense anxiety while you are there, typically remaining in the background or keeping as 'hidden' as possible. What you fear is that you will be embarrassed or humiliated by what you will reveal to others.

The terminology that is used in describing several of the criteria is somewhat general and the need for exercising clinical judgement is evident, for example in deciding what constitutes significant interference with normal routine or what is meant by 'almost invariably'. In chapter 6 we look more closely at the effects of anxiety upon the quality of the person's life. We consider the degree of impairment in the person's ability to function effectively in life. We take into account the amount of distress that he or she experiences.

There are criteria for exclusion as well as for inclusion. A condition is not classified as Social Anxiety Disorder if the signs that are presented can be explained in terms of another condition. It is important for the clinician to determine whether the signs might be better understood as belonging to another condition, whether this is a response to a physical condition (as in the example of fear of trembling associated with Parkinson's disease) or another psychological condition. We shall see shortly that social anxiety disorder is frequently associated with depression, general anxiety or alcohol problems. It is important too that the clinician explores the life circumstances of the patient. Are these anxieties related to a change in employment, taking on additional responsibilities, or to conditions in the workplace, for example being bullied or harassed?

The final statement in the list refers to the specification of generalized social phobia. The distinction between generalized and non-generalized social phobia was introduced in the revision of the manual that was published in 1987. This is an example of a change brought about by increased knowledge of the condition that followed research. Evidence had not supported the claim made in the early editions of the manual that an individual who is suffering from social phobia tends to have fears about a single type of situation, for example one person might have fears about public speaking, another about dating, yet another about eating in public, and so on. Many individuals report anxieties about a wide range of different social situations. Accordingly, subsequent editions of the manual have adjusted the criteria to incorporate anxiety about one or more types of social situations. The distinction has implications for treatment, as we explain in later chapters. A specific fear, for example stage fright or performance anxiety, the fear experienced by a musician, actor or public speaker, might be amenable to treatment by anti-anxiety drugs such as beta blockers or benzodiazepines which can be taken about thirty minutes to an hour before the performance. This medication is targeted at performance on a specific occasion and it would not be helpful (indeed it could lead to dependence problems) if it were used whenever anxiety was regularly experienced in a range of routine situations.

## Do I suffer from social anxiety disorder?

A list of criteria is not necessarily helpful if we wish to discover whether our difficulties fall into the range where a diagnosis of social anxiety disorder might be applied. In chapter 6 we shall discuss the degree of impairment and distress as factors in the need for treatment. Several self-rating questionnaires have been constructed, as a screening assessment or for use in clinical research and in epidemiological surveys of social anxiety disorder in the general population. Box 2 displays the items

## Box 2: Social Phobia Inventory (SPIN)

Each item is to be rated on a five-point scale:

0 = not at all
1 = a little bit
2 = somewhat
3 = very much
4 = extremely

1. Fear of people in authority
2. Bothered by blushing
3. Fear of parties and social events
4. Avoids talking to strangers
5. Fear of criticism
6. Avoids embarrassment
7. Distressed by sweating
8. Avoids parties
9. Avoids being the centre of attention
10. Fear of talking to strangers
11. Avoids speeches
12. Avoids criticism
13. Distressed by palpitations
14. Fear of others watching
15. Fear of embarrassment
16. Avoids talking to authority figures
17. Distressed by trembling or shaking

Source: Connor, K. M., Davidson, J. R. T., Churchill, L. E., Sherwood, A., Foa, E. B., and Weisler, R. H. (2000). Psychometric properties of the Social Phobia Inventory (SPIN): a new self-rating scale. *British Journal of Psychiatry*, 176, 379–386. Reproduced by permission of the Royal College of Psychiatrists.

of the Social Phobia Inventory (SPIN), a self-rating screening assessment questionnaire constructed by Connor and her associates. This is designed to be completed by the individual on their own. Each of the seventeen items is answered on a five-point scale. For example, if you believe that you have an extreme fear of authority, you would answer '4' to this item; if you were not bothered at all by blushing you would answer '0' to item 2, and so on. You might wish to complete this questionnaire.

The item content refers to fear and avoidance of certain kinds of social situations. Items also refer to being distressed by physiological reactions including blushing, sweating, trembling and palpitations. The situations and reactions are familiar to us from the first chapters of this book. They are also characteristic of shyness and are mentioned in items in shyness questionnaires. Notably they do not refer to the 'excessive or unreasonable' nature of the fear or the intense anxiety or panic that is experienced in the feared situations, even though excessiveness and intensity of reaction are thought to distinguish between shyness and social phobia.

Scores on the items can be added to give a total score, which would range from zero to sixty-eight. However, the questionnaire is easier to interpret if average scores are considered or we count the frequency of items that attract a high rating. An average item score can be calculated by dividing the total score by seventeen. The middle score for each item would be two so we could count the number of items where the rating is higher than two.

Scores can be interpreted by reference to the scores obtained by samples of people who meet criteria for social anxiety or social anxiety disorder. In developing the questionnaire the scores obtained by patients undergoing treatment for social phobia and social anxiety disorder were compared with a control group. This group comprised samples of patients who were diagnosed with medical or psychiatric conditions other than social phobia. Such comparisons enable us to interpret our scores on the questionnaire.

How many items did you answer with a rating of either three or four? The frequency differed markedly between social anxiety and control groups in the development study. Between twenty-eight per cent and eighty-six per cent of the social anxiety sample made ratings of at least three on the items. On the other hand, less than ten per cent of the control group scored three or four on any of the items. (There was one exception, item eleven, 'avoids speeches', as seventeen per cent of the control group reported very much or extreme anxiety on this item. Even though this is relatively high – most of us find public speaking daunting – it contrasts with the eighty-six of the social anxiety disorder sample who provided ratings of at least three on this item.)

Scores can also be compared in terms of averages. The anxiety group's average rating for an item was 2.4; this represents a rating that falls between 'somewhat' and 'very much'. The average for the control group was 0.6, falling between 'not at all' and a 'little bit'.

In summary, the more items that you answer with a rating of three or four or if your average item score is greater than two this shows that your answers to the questionnaire are more similar to those obtained by a sample who have been diagnosed with generalized social anxiety disorder than they are to answers from a sample who do not meet this diagnosis.

*Scores on questionnaires like these have to be treated with caution.*

The questionnaire has been developed as a brief screening tool and cannot claim to be an accurate 'measure' of social anxiety disorder or provide reliable signs that an individual scoring above the cut-off 'has' a social anxiety disorder. Diagnosis would require a much more intensive assessment which would collect more detailed information from the individual about his or her life, including any other anxieties and problems that they are experiencing. As we saw in the diagnostic criteria other causes of the individual's problems have to be excluded. We return to this issue in chapter 6.

Also, the scores of the 'control group' are relatively low, given the responses that samples of people make to shyness questionnaires. Anxieties about the kinds of situations included in the social phobia scale are common, as we have seen in chapter 2; scores on the questionnaire might underestimate levels of social anxiety in the non-clinical population.

The items in the questionnaires are very similar in content to the items in shyness questionnaires and the lists of situations that shy people find difficult. They refer to symptoms such as blushing, sweating, and trembling that cause shy people concern. This confirms the considerable overlap between shyness and social anxiety. However, there is no gain in replacing one label – 'shyness' – by another – 'social anxiety disorder'. The more likely you are to obtain scores on a questionnaire that are suggestive of shyness or anxiety the more you are identifying concerns in your own life. The first question to ask is whether you wish to change these aspects of your life. If you do, the next question is how to do this. This book sets out several directions you could take but which one you decide to take is your choice, though this is a decision that you might wish to make with the advice of friends or professionals. The important thing is that you want to change, and are not persuaded to do so because you think that you ought to change, whether this is through direct influence by others or through more diffuse pressure from the media and other public sources of information that imply that shyness is a problem or an illness. We discuss how to change in the next chapters.

## What does research into social anxiety tell us?

There has been a rapid growth in clinical research into social anxiety disorder since the 1980s. Some of this research refers to social phobia rather than to social anxiety disorder because it preceded the change in terminology. To avoid confusion we use the term social anxiety disorder when describing the research. This research has produced a number of important findings that we summarize briefly here.

- The incidence of social anxiety disorder in the general population is high. It is believed to affect about thirteen per cent of the population at some time in their life. It is estimated to be the third most common psychiatric disorder in the United States, after major depression (seventeen per cent lifetime prevalence) and alcohol dependence (fourteen per cent). A random survey of the population that was undertaken in Sweden concluded that sixteen per cent of their sample met the criteria for social phobia. Clearly many people who meet diagnostic criteria for social anxiety disorder do not receive medical treatment: one study estimated that only three per cent of diagnosed cases had received treatment within the preceding year.
- It is a chronic disorder. One study showed that the average duration of the disorder is twenty-five years and in some cases it lasted as long as forty-five years. It does not seem to be the case that extreme anxiety disappears by itself. One reason for this is that so few people receive treatment. Most people learn to cope with their anxiety. This can be done but often at the expense of the quality of their life, as we report throughout this book. The coping strategies that people adopt – including 'safety behaviours' as we describe in several chapters – are limiting. Not only do they reduce the quality of social experiences; they also deny us the chance to learn. If I believe that speaking up in front of others will reveal me to be inadequate I miss many opportunities for advancement or for personal satisfaction. At the same time I have no way of disproving this belief, of finding that people do value me and my contributions.

- It is more common among women than among men. It is not clear why this should be, since there do not seem to be differences between men and women in the incidence of shyness. It could be that women are more likely to seek professional help or to be diagnosed.
- Individuals who are diagnosed with one medical condition often meet the diagnostic criteria for other conditions as well. The technical term for this association between conditions is *comorbidity*. Social anxiety disorder is comorbid with depression and alcohol abuse: patients in treatment for social anxiety disorder are diagnosed with major depression and alcohol problems in fifteen to twenty per cent of cases. Approximately one in four people with social anxiety disorder is significantly depressed.
- Comorbidity with depression is consistent with evidence that shy and socially anxious individuals have low self-esteem and little confidence in themselves. The impact of social anxiety on limiting the quality of life must surely be a factor too, particularly as the shy and socially anxious blame themselves for their difficulties. Comorbidity is also consistent with evidence that social anxiety disorder is associated with somewhat higher rates of attempted suicide. The association with alcohol problems is not surprising, as research has shown that individuals with shyness and social anxiety frequently use alcohol as a way of trying to cope with social situations. As we noted earlier, as many as twenty per cent of people with social anxiety disorder rely on alcohol to manage their anxiety. A survey by shyness researcher Bernardo J. Carducci identified the following illustrative quotations from a sample of college students:

Since I'm in college now, most of the social functions involve alcohol. I admit I use it as a social lubricant.

If there is a social function with a large group of people I'm uncomfortable with, I will not go unless there is alcohol.

I do like drinking with my friends, but I notice that I tend to indulge myself in alcohol to feel more loose and talkative when it comes to meeting my boyfriend's friends. But then when I see them sober, I feel like a loser because they just saw me the other night as a happy talkative drunk.

The prop that alcohol provides is clearly only temporary and frequent reliance upon it makes the socially anxious vulnerable to dependence and the problems that this adds to their anxieties. Chapter 9 discusses the implications of reliance on alcohol or drugs for treatment. Substance dependence can create additional problems and interfere with standard treatments. People with social anxiety disorder who drink or use drugs may require treatment that can address both problems simultaneously.

- Social anxiety has a marked impact on the life of those who suffer from it. Their fears and their tendency to avoid social interactions can severely impede their social functioning, making even routine situations such as eating in a restaurant or ordering a drink something to be dreaded. It can lead to unsatisfying social relationships, to loneliness and social isolation.
- It affects children as well as adults. The prevalence in the general child population is estimated as between one and two per cent. Social anxiety disorder is one of the most common disorders of childhood: one study has reported that the fears of one in every five children who attend an anxiety clinic are social fears. The average age of onset is in adolescence, though studies have identified children as young as eight years who meet the diagnostic criteria. The diagnosis of children's psychological problems requires particular care,

expertise, and experience on the part of the clinician. The clinician has to take into account what children of a given age can be expected to be able to do at that age. For example, it is common for young children to go through a phase where they shrink from strangers. Another difficulty in diagnosis is that the child's difficulties may only become apparent when impairment of functioning becomes evident; distress and difficulties in relationships may only be noticed when the child faces particular challenges in growing up, such as forming friendships, moving from one school to another, facing more demanding tasks in school, and forming intimate relationships. The anxiety and distress might have been there for a long time without being noticed by parents or teachers. Social anxiety has been shown to be comorbid with other disorders in childhood. It is associated with other anxiety disorders and with depression.

- What are the causes of social anxiety disorder? This is a difficult question to answer and requires much more research before a definitive answer can be given. There is evidence that genetic factors play a part. We have seen in chapter 4 that reactivity in infancy and inhibited temperament in early childhood predict later shyness, social anxiety disorder, and other anxiety disorders later in childhood and in adulthood. Nevertheless, genetic factors and innate temperament are only the beginning of a journey. They may make a child more vulnerable to later problems but whether these problems do emerge depends on many factors. Parenting is one of them: parents who are supportive but who are not overprotective of their child can help a vulnerable child towards happier outcomes. Overprotectiveness is not helpful for vulnerable children and may maintain their shyness and anxiety as they lack opportunities to confront their fears and learn from them. Fortunately, treatment for social anxiety disorder can be successful for children and adults as they present their fears and symptoms; detailed knowledge of the origins of problems is not essential for treating them effectively.

- Finally, controlled clinical studies have shown that social anxiety disorder is amenable to treatment. This is an important finding, and we discuss the forms of treatment and the evidence for their effectiveness in later chapters.

## Key points

- The diagnosis of a psychological condition is a matter of clinical judgement in the light of knowledge about the condition, knowledge that increases over time. Evidence about the effects of particular treatments also influences clinicians' views on the treatments that are available.
- The history of social phobia shows how understanding of this condition has changed significantly within a relatively short period of time. Currently social anxiety disorder is identified as a potentially serious condition that causes distress and is associated with impairment of effective social functioning.
- Diagnostic criteria have been developed for social anxiety disorder. These refer to excessive and persistent fear of social situations that interfere with the individual's routine functioning. Fear of showing signs of anxiety contributes to social anxiety.
- Avoidant personality disorder has been identified as a separate disorder that shares many aspects of extreme shyness and social anxiety. It is defined in terms of inhibited social behaviour, feelings of inadequacy, and sensitivity to being evaluated and criticized by others. Its relation to social anxiety disorder is not fully understood.
- The diagnostic criteria of social anxiety disorder and avoidant personality disorder seem to have much in common with

the experience, symptoms and consequences of shyness. The relations among these are not fully understood. One plausible conjecture is that they vary along a dimension of severity, with avoidant personality disorder involving the greatest anxiety.

- Self-rating scales have been developed for screening purposes and for carrying out surveys into the prevalence of social anxiety in the population. A short scale is presented in the chapter. Interpretation of scores should be treated with caution. While they show an individual roughly where they stand with regard to other people, a diagnosis of a condition that would benefit from treatment requires a more careful and detailed examination of each individual case.
- Research, often using such scales, indicates that the incidence of social anxiety disorder in the population is high.
- Social anxiety disorder can be a serious and long-lasting condition.
- Social anxiety disorder is frequently associated with alcohol reliance and depression.
- Social anxiety disorder can be identified in children and young people. It can be serious for this age group too, with problems of comorbidity. Diagnosis can be particularly difficult with young children and requires sensitivity and specialist knowledge on the part of the clinician.
- Despite the seriousness of the condition, treatment for social anxiety disorder can be effective.

# 6

# Is treatment for you?

## How do you know if you need treatment?

It is difficult for socially anxious people to recognize when treatment would be useful. For one thing, as we noted in chapter 4, social anxiety often begins in childhood or early adolescence. As we encounter life experiences and our personality evolves, social anxiety can become interwoven with other aspects of our experience and blend into our sense of self-identity ('it's just the way I am'). Another factor that obscures the recognition that treatment would be useful is that social anxiety is part of the human experience. As discussed throughout the book, most people are shy or anxious in at least some social situations. We suggest that it helps us to understand social anxiety if we recognize that there is a dimension of severity. There is no clear division between shyness or social anxiety as a common, shared human experience and social anxiety disorder (SAD), a clinical condition that requires treatment. Family and friends also have difficulty recognizing when

## Box 1: Anxiety – a dimension of severity

| Normal social anxiety | Social anxiety disorder |
|---|---|
| Anxious before date with new person | Turns down dates or seldom dates for fear of rejection |
| Anxious when promoted to supervisory position | Turns down promotion due to anxiety and fear of being criticized |
| Uncomfortable when returning purchase to shop | Will not enter shop if only person; keeps unsatisfactory merchandise |
| Gets butterflies when giving a talk in class | Drops out of classes that involve giving oral presentations or group interactions |
| Feels apprehensive before giving an important presentation at work | Tries to avoid presentations; speaks softly and avoids eye contact when speaking to work groups |

therapy would be helpful. Family members, in particular, frequently try to reassure socially anxious people that there is nothing wrong with them and that they simply need to push themselves to break out of their shell.

Even when social anxiety is recognized as causing impairment and distress, people may avoid seeking treatment. People with SAD tend to view their anxiety as an embarrassing personal defect and are reluctant to talk about it with their doctors or other health professionals. Therefore, they fail to initiate a treatment referral. They are also embarrassed to contact a therapist or to be seen participating in therapy. Even when they arrange to attend a treatment programme, they are reluctant to be seen entering the building or therapy room. Some arrive at the treatment centre and immediately leave because their anxiety is too great or because they feel humiliated to be there.

Personal reluctance to seek treatment is further complicated by the fact that relatively few doctors and other health care professionals have sufficient experience or training to diagnose SAD. Indeed, many doctors do not ask their patients about SAD despite the prevalence and impact of this condition. In addition, they often fail to recognize that SAD is the problem even when patients report emotional symptoms. Misdiagnosis is not uncommon. Socially anxious people can be incorrectly diagnosed as having panic disorder, depression, or general anxiety. Therefore, it often falls to the socially anxious person to decide if and where to seek treatment. All of these factors act together to prevent the person from obtaining therapy. It is sobering to note that nearly two-thirds of people with SAD do not receive treatment. Of the one-third who do, there can be a delay, perhaps of years, in reaching specialist care, that is, a knowledgeable therapist. This is unfortunate because effective treatments for social anxiety disorder do exist and have helped many people overcome disabling social anxiety. In this chapter, we hope to provide guidance for when and how to obtain treatment.

## Deciding to seek treatment

How do you determine whether treatment is needed? Professionals use two criteria to make this judgement, impairment and distress. To these professional criteria, we add lowered quality of life. People require treatment when SAD causes significant life impairment, produces severe distress, or lowers their overall sense of happiness and satisfaction with life.

### Impairment

Impairment refers to a reduction in our ability to function effectively. Because most activities involve other people, social anxiety can interfere with a wide range of situations.

Box 2: Impairment

*Social*
Few close friends
Few or no romantic relationships
Rarely socializes
Lives with family members or alone due to anxiety
Avoids sexual contact

*Work and school*
Avoids courses that require group discussion or oral presentations
Unwilling to contact lecturer or teacher for guidance
Avoids careers that require social contact
Failure to progress in job due to anxiety
Refuses promotions
Unable to attend work-related social events

*Leisure activities*
Has no hobbies or interests outside work
Sticks to a routine – new activities avoided
Unwilling to go to gyms, fitness centres, or other exercise programmes due to anxiety

*Daily functioning*
Minimizes being in public places
Difficulty dealing with shop assistants
Avoids answering or talking on telephone

*Health*
Frequent colds and flu
Avoids talking with family doctor
Muscle tension and headaches

*Economic*
Underemployed
Unemployed

SOCIAL RELATIONSHIPS

One of the most common reasons for seeking treatment is when social anxiety hinders our development of friendships and romantic relationships. To evaluate social impairment, you should ask yourself whether you are satisfied with the *quality* of your friendships. The most important determinant of social satisfaction is not the sheer number of friends or social activities, but rather that you have people who can be counted on for help and support. Some socially anxious individuals participate in weekly social activities, but their interactions remain at a superficial level. With true friendship, we feel that we can be ourselves. We can be spontaneous and genuine, rather than cautious and artificial. The same considerations enter into romantic relationships. Key questions here are whether dating relationships persist and deepen over time. The absence of dating or romantic relationships, or having many fewer relationships than peers because of social anxiety, is an important cue that treatment might be helpful. Another sign is if relationships always sputter out after a few dates due to anxiety or avoidance.

## SCHOOL AND COLLEGE PERFORMANCE

The effect of social anxiety on school and college performance has only recently received the attention it deserves. Common signs of impairment at school or college are if you feel unable to speak in class, avoid verbal presentations or participation in group assignments, and base career decisions on a perceived need to avoid social interactions rather than on personal interest. Another sign that social anxiety is problematic is if you are reluctant to seek help from teachers and other students, and therefore miss out on important information. Although many students are anxious in the company of their teachers, students with SAD will not approach them even when they are failing. Similarly, most students are tense or anxious during exams because they are motivated to perform well. Severe test anxiety, however, can be a result of SAD. In this case, the person is so concerned about evaluation that he or she freezes during exams and receives low marks despite having adequate intellectual ability and having prepared well for the exam. If you experience any of these difficulties, you

## Case 1

> Marion was teased by her male classmates during high school and developed the belief that men found her unattractive and would make fun of her, especially if they thought she was interested in them. At college, she found that she would avoid men whom she found attractive, although she had no difficulty talking with men who were of less interest to her. Even if an attractive man displayed interest in her, she gave brief responses and ended the interaction as soon as she could. In her final year, she recognized that her women friends had developed serious relationships and several had married, while she remained alone. She decided to get treatment to overcome her dating fears.

should seriously consider getting treatment before entering the workforce. Students with SAD who suffer test anxiety or public speaking fears also should be encouraged to seek advice.

Unfortunately, in the United Kingdom at least, opportunities to find help may be limited during the early school years. Shy and anxious students may never draw attention to themselves because their quiet and conformist behaviour presents no problems to the class teacher who typically has to give more attention to noisy or disruptive students. If shy children perform adequately in their school work, they are likely to remain 'invisible'. Consequently the school will see no need to draw the attention of the child's parents to their child's behaviour. Shy children can be victims of bullying and this might attract the school's attention. Even here, however, the child may not admit to being bullied or teachers and parents might not make the connection between the bullying and the child's social anxiety. There are greater opportunities for college students to explore whether their college offers treatment for these common problems through their student counselling centre. Most further and higher education institutions have this resource. Many students will seek help from their counselling centre if they are anxious about their academic work or about financial or housing problems. However, these centres also provide support for students who experience anxiety about giving presentations and speaking up in front of others as well as for interpersonal problems more generally. Students can be helped with any problem that interferes with the quality of their student life and this help is given in confidence. Nothing is shared with teachers without the student's permission.

Treatment is more likely to be effective the earlier you begin. Another advantage of seeking treatment during your school years is that schools and colleges provide ample opportunity for social interaction and developing social relationships. Therefore, skills learned in treatment can be readily implemented. In addition, you will not miss out on important social developmental learning. These are prime years for you to learn how to relate to and work with others, as well as how to manage romantic attachments. Do not be discouraged, however, if your school days are behind you. Research indicates that treatment can be effective at any age. The important factor is to acknowledge that social anxiety is a problem and seek treatment.

WORKPLACE FUNCTIONING

The effect of social anxiety in the workplace is also important. Signs that social anxiety may impair your work performance are if you are reluctant to present ideas in group meetings or speak with supervisors, fail to receive credit for accomplishments because you avoid the spotlight, and refuse promotions or job assignments that require social interaction or supervisory responsibilities. Subtle signs of impairment include reluctance to talk on the telephone and reliance on email communication rather than the face-to-face interaction that has been shown to enhance career success. Another important indicator of impairment is if you avoid workplace social activities due to anxiety. Such avoidance reduces opportunities to network and to develop the personal relationships needed to do well at work. Difficulty obtaining jobs due to social anxiety is a very important sign that treatment is needed.

## Case 2

Edward had been a good student at university and obtained a responsible position as a laboratory technician after graduation. He felt quite anxious around his co-workers because he felt that he was less knowledgeable and skilful than they were. After the first awkward introductions, he avoided talking with them unless absolutely necessary, and then confined his comments to work requests. He turned down their initial invitations to go out for drinks after work, and eventually they stopped inviting him. His pattern was to enter the lab quietly, go to his work station, work quietly by himself all day, and avoid making eye contact with his co-workers even when discussing work matters. When his discomfort persisted even after two years, he decided that he needed help to overcome his social anxiety.

## Case 3

William had been painfully shy as a child, but managed to complete high school and a technical training course, and took a position on a railway maintenance crew. He married a woman who had actively pursued him and they had a child. Although William felt anxious at work, his technical skills were good and he was well regarded by his co-workers. When their team supervisor left, the manager wanted to promote William to the position. Although his co-workers were enthusiastic about the promotion, he became preoccupied with the fear that he would not be able to make good decisions and would be ridiculed by his mates. Therefore, he refused the promotion. When his co-workers expressed their disappointment, he felt foolish and stopped going to the pub with them after work. Shortly thereafter his wife left him, and he felt unable to meet other women because he considered himself to be a failure. At this point, he recognized that his social anxiety and avoidance was shrinking his life and sought treatment.

### LEISURE ACTIVITIES

Although we do not often think about impairment in hobbies and leisure activities as stemming from social anxiety, SAD can also limit your functioning in these areas. If social anxiety prevents you from going to the gym or fitness classes or participating in leisure activities that involve groups, such as taking cooking courses or dance classes or participating in volunteer activities, you may do well to seek treatment.

### ACTIVITIES OF DAILY LIVING

Signs of impairment in routine activities of daily living include buying articles you do not want due to fears of refusing sales assistants, and trouble signing your name in public or eating in restaurants due to fear that others will see that you are trembling. A person's ability to drive can even be affected by fears of offending or inconveniencing others.

### HEALTH

Social anxiety can impair your health if it interferes with going to the doctor or talking about symptoms of significant diseases. Certainly the presence of those problems would suggest that treatment is warranted.

## Distress

A second criterion for determining whether treatment would be useful is distress. Some people with SAD do not avoid social events but rather experience severe distress during those events. They may force themselves to engage in social activities, and even handle them skilfully, but feel painfully self-conscious and uncomfortable. Therefore, they do not take pleasure in the company of others. Social events become ordeals to be endured rather than interesting and rewarding experiences. For example, one computer expert gave clear and helpful presentations at work, but felt so uncomfortable while doing so that he always concluded that he had done a poor job, even when he received positive feedback. Another man forced himself to attend a singles' dance. He saw a woman that he found attractive, asked her to dance, and she accepted. Although they danced well together and had much to talk about, he felt so uncomfortable that he refused her invitation for a second dance because he believed that she simply 'felt sorry' for him. In this case, the problem is not so much that you are impaired by avoidance or constriction, but rather that extreme anxiety deprives you of recognizing your accomplishments and causes misery rather than enjoyment.

### Quality of life

Quality of life refers to the person's general satisfaction with life. One indication that social anxiety requires treatment is if you feel that you are drifting along in a state of vague unhappiness with the sense that life is meaningless or deficient. Much of our personal identity comes from our relationships with other people. Research also shows that having social relationships increases positive emotion, that is, our general level of happiness, joy and curiosity. Indeed, one of the most effective ways of increasing such positive emotions is to interact with other people. Positive emotion in turn, makes us feel more sociable and more positive about people around us. Thus, social contact and positive emotions interact in a self-perpetuating cycle. When social anxiety hinders the development of social relationships and participation in meaningful activities, life becomes dull and unrewarding. A chronic lack of life satisfaction and the absence of pleasure and happiness can be a signal that you would benefit from treatment.

## What types of treatment are available?

Once you decide that social anxiety causes significant impairment and distress, or lowers your life satisfaction, you must decide what type of treatment would be useful. Treatment for SAD can be divided into two categories, psychological treatments (psychotherapy) and pharmacological treatments (pharmacotherapy, medication). Here, we will briefly describe various treatment options. In chapters 7 and 8, we will discuss cognitive behavioural therapy in more detail, and in chapter 9, we will talk about medications that are used to treat social anxiety.

## Psychological therapies

These are therapies that use psychological techniques to help people understand their emotional problems better and develop more effective ways to handle them. These therapies typically involve discussion with a trained professional and participation in activities that teach new ways to view or respond to negative emotions and life situations. While different approaches to therapy use somewhat different techniques to accomplish those goals, all of these approaches emphasize the importance of a collaborative relationship between the therapist and patient, the need to arrive at a clear understanding of the patient's situation, and encouragement to take an alternative perspective on one's problems.

### COGNITIVE BEHAVIOURAL THERAPY (CBT)

CBT is the most frequently used psychological therapy. As with other psychological treatments, CBT occurs within the context of a supportive collaborative relationship and encourages the person to take a new perspective on their social anxiety and interpersonal behaviour. CBT places particular emphasis on the way that we think about social situations, including our beliefs about and expectations for social events. According to this perspective, socially anxious people's social predictions and interpretations are overly negative. The goal of treatment therefore is to correct these negative thought patterns. With CBT, people are encouraged to conduct *behavioural experiments* to evaluate their social predictions and beliefs and then to correct any inaccuracies.

CBT is a short-term treatment that typically consists of twelve to twenty weekly sessions. Treatment focuses on current social events and behaviour, rather than the historical causes of social anxiety. In contrast to traditional talk therapies, CBT uses structured activities aimed at accomplishing specific goals. To be effective, you will need to devote time between sessions applying the techniques presented. CBT can be provided in either group or individual format. The effectiveness of CBT is supported by numerous scientific studies. The advantages of CBT programmes over pharmacotherapy are that treatment gains are likely to be maintained after treatment is completed and the side effects of medication are avoided. The disadvantages are that treatment requires specialized treatment providers and you must be willing to devote time to weekly sessions and between-session exercises. In addition, CBT typically takes somewhat longer to produce effects than medication. CBT is discussed in greater detail in chapters 7 and 8.

SOCIAL SKILLS TRAINING (SST)

SST is a form of behaviour therapy that was widely used prior to the development of current CBT programmes. Whereas CBT focuses on the role of negative thinking in social anxiety, SST is based on the idea that social anxiety arises from deficiencies in social skills. According to this perspective, social anxiety and negative thinking arise because people with SAD correctly recognize that their behaviour is inadequate. Thus, the key to overcoming anxiety and negative thinking is to develop more effective social behaviour. Socially anxious people do in fact report that they do not know how to behave and that their behaviour is awkward and unskilled. It is not yet clear however, whether those judgements are accurate or reflect overly negative thinking.

In SST programmes, therapists describe and demonstrate skills for handling problem situations. Participants rehearse these skills during sessions and receive feedback on their performance, sometimes through observing videotapes of themselves role playing problem situations. Just as in CBT, participants are asked to practise their newly learned skills between sessions. The goal of these exercises, however, is to master more effective social behaviour rather than to correct mistaken beliefs and predictions.

As with CBT, SST is a short-term, structured treatment that is typically presented in weekly sessions, often conducted in a group format. The effectiveness of SST has been supported by scientific studies. SST produces the same pattern of gradual improvement over twelve to twenty treatment sessions as that found in CBT. Although some studies have found that CBT is more effective than SST, most studies that have compared the two treatments find they are equally effective. As with CBT, the disadvantages of SST are that it requires specialized treatment providers, participants have to devote time and effort to weekly sessions and between-session exercises, and treatment takes longer to produce effects than medication. On the positive side, SST produces significant changes in anxiety symptoms and behaviour, and those gains are more likely to be maintained after treatment is over.

SPECIFIC SKILL WORKSHOPS

There are a variety of programmes that teach specific social skills. Examples include courses and workshops on public speaking and assertiveness. In addition, workshops teaching leadership skills and negotiation tactics can be helpful for the socially anxious person. Specific skill workshops are often offered through community colleges, work settings, or private companies. Specific skill training workshops generally follow a SST format. Workshop leaders describe and demonstrate skills.

Then, participants rehearse those skills in session and apply what they have learned between sessions. Evaluation studies indicate that such programmes can be effective in helping socially anxious people master specific skill areas if the programme is offered by knowledgeable leaders and is of sufficient duration to allow skill mastery. To achieve benefits, you must faithfully and repeatedly apply what you have learned to your daily life. Mere attendance is seldom enough to produce sustained change.

## GRADUATED EXPOSURE (GE)

GE is another early form of behaviour therapy. This treatment is based on the principle of *anxiety habituation* – the fact that in the absence of any true danger, anxiety naturally fades over time. The goal of GE is to encourage socially anxious people to approach feared situations in a stepwise, or gradual, manner, beginning with the least anxiety-provoking and moving up to more anxiety-provoking events. The person is required to remain in the situation until anxiety naturally declines. With repeated *exposures*, the situation no longer causes significant anxiety, and the person can move on to the next step. GE is sometimes combined with training in relaxation strategies. One such strategy is *progressive muscle relaxation* (PMR) in which you learn to release muscle tension through a series of exercises that involve tensing and relaxing various muscle groups. Another relaxation strategy is autogenic training, which is based on self-hypnosis and involves learning to tune into and increase natural body sensations associated with a state of relaxation. You can then use the relaxation strategy when entering anxiety-provoking situations.

GE has been evaluated scientifically and found to produce significant reductions in social anxiety and avoidance. For many years, it was considered as effective as any other type of behavioural or cognitive therapy. More recent versions of CBT, however, have been found to produce greater benefits. The principle underlying GE, gradual approach and prolonged exposure, is often incorporated in other treatment approaches, where it is combined with CBT or SST techniques.

## MINDFULNESS-BASED COGNITIVE THERAPY (MBCT)

Since the 1980s there has been growing interest in the development of techniques that encourage acceptance rather than control of anxiety and other negative emotional states. MBCT is based on the Buddhist philosophy of living in the present moment. Eastern therapies, such as Japanese *Morita Therapy*, encourage people to recognize that emotions and thoughts are natural phenomena that cannot be directly controlled or changed through acts of will. Indeed, Eastern therapists believe that attempts to control internal states are counterproductive because they maintain an unhealthy self-centredness. Instead, they encourage people to be *mindful* of thoughts and accept them without judgement, and then to lose one's self through 'constructive action', that is, doing things that are positive for society. Moritian therapists who work with socially anxious people encourage them to 'accept reality' (*arugamama*) and choose to lead a constructive life despite uncertainties, fears, and conflicts ('take anxious action').

MBCT is based on Western versions of these Eastern views and uses mindfulness techniques without the overlay of Buddhist spiritual philosophy. MBCT programmes usually consist of eight weekly two-hour classes with weekly assignments to be completed outside the sessions. The aim of the programme is to enhance awareness of thoughts and feelings so that you can respond to situations with choice rather than reacting automatically. Whereas CBT focuses on correcting negative distortions in thinking, MBCT teaches the process of attending to thoughts and feelings without judgement or trying to change them. The goal is to prevent you from getting drawn into automatic thoughts and patterns. MBCT has been shown to be effective in preventing relapse in severe depression, helping people manage pain, and reducing general anxiety. Formal evaluations with SAD are just beginning, but clinical reports indicate that some people with SAD find mindfulness training useful. MBCT is most often incorporated into a broader CBT treatment programme.

PSYCHODYNAMIC THERAPY

Psychodynamic therapy is also referred to as dynamic or analytical therapy. This approach is a traditional form of talk therapy that focuses on the psychological conflicts and motives that underlie social anxiety. In contrast to CBT and other forms of behaviour therapy, dynamic therapists work to identify the social developmental experiences that contributed to the onset of the person's social fears and to understand how those experiences continue to affect current behaviour and relationships. People are encouraged to *work through* (understand and come to peace with) the life events that contributed to their social fears. Dynamic therapy is most often used for severe anxiety and avoidance. Treatment is provided through weekly individual therapy sessions with highly trained psychiatrists or psychologists. Dynamic treatment can be beneficial for socially anxious people. However, research shows that on average, it is significantly less effective than either CBT or pharmacotherapy and takes longer to produce improvement.

PHARMACOTHERAPY (PT)

The most widely used form of treatment for social anxiety and SAD is pharmacotherapy. In PT, medication is used to reduce physical symptoms of fear and anxiety. For Generalized SAD, the most frequently used medications are the Serotonin Reuptake Inhibitors (SSRIs and NSRIs). Medication is delivered through daily tablets taken for a number of months and often for several years. Severely anxious people may stay on medication for longer periods of time. Although these medications do not work for everyone, when they do work, they often reduce social anxiety symptoms fairly quickly (six to eight weeks). If SRIs are not effective, other medications for generalized SAD are available. Short-term anti-anxiety medications are sometimes used for people with severe performance anxieties, such as musicians. Here, medication is taken on a situational basis prior to the event in order to block anxiety reactions.

Medication is generally prescribed by family doctors or psychiatrists. The advantages of pharmacotherapy are that it requires little patient time and effort, is widely available, and can produce rapid symptom change. The disadvantages are that medication can produce side effects, the person may need to remain on medication for a long period of time, and treatment benefits can disappear when medication is discontinued. Relapse rates tend to be higher for medication than CBT regimens. Pharmacotherapy is discussed in greater detail in chapter 9.

## Other approaches to change

### Self-help workbooks

A number of experienced therapists have written self-help workbooks for people with SAD. These workbooks provide step by step guides that you can follow to overcome your anxiety and avoidance. Most self-help guides are based on CBT, SST, and GE techniques and include worksheets and structured exercises. The advantages of self-help workbooks are the convenience and privacy of being able to use them at home and at your own pace. The disadvantages are that the negative thinking that often accompanies SAD can prevent you from accurately assessing yourself and recognizing your own strengths and successes. In addition, you must be highly motivated to apply the exercises without structure and guidance, and unfortunately, non-compliance is common. Self-help workbooks can be useful, particularly if they are combined with brief contact with trained therapists, either in person or on the telephone. Although treatment with therapists is believed to be more effective than self-help manuals alone, these books can provide treatment in geographical locations where trained therapists are unavailable. They are often a good way for people to learn about social anxiety and to begin to understand the principles for overcoming it.

## Internet forums

The availability of the Internet has opened up new possibilities for people with SAD. Internet forums, or chat rooms, have been developed specifically for socially anxious people. These chat rooms offer the opportunity for you to share your experiences with social anxiety and to receive suggestions and support from other socially anxious people. Some professionals initially expressed concerns that Internet forums might become a substitute for face-to-face interaction and unwittingly increase social avoidance. Those fears have not been confirmed. Socially anxious people do not appear to spend more time on the Internet than other people. There is no indication that Internet use decreases social contacts. Socially anxious people may use the Internet differently than others, however. Outgoing people report that they use the Internet to keep in touch with their family and friends and to facilitate face-to-face interactions. Shy and introverted people, in contrast, report that they communicate online to avoid being alone and are more likely to communicate with people with whom they do not have close relationships.

The research evidence about Internet forums is mixed. On the negative side, socially anxious people also fear negative evaluation on their electronic communications and are more often passive observers rather than active participants in these forums. In addition, Internet use was found to strengthen maladaptive beliefs, in particular the belief that socially anxious people lack social skills and that others are likely to criticize them. On the positive side, people with SAD report that the Internet provided them with new information about social anxiety and increased their awareness that SAD is treatable. Furthermore, people who live in remote areas or who are too anxious and avoidant to talk with their doctor or treatment centres can now learn about SAD as a condition and about treatment possibilities. They can also contact anxiety disorders associations and specialized anxiety disorder treatment centres to identify therapists and treatment programmes in their area. Indeed, surveys indicate that people who contact treatment centres electronically are more severely avoidant than those who are in treatment programmes. This pattern suggests that there is a group of severely anxious people whose needs are not being met through conventional treatment programmes.

An exciting new approach that might meet the needs of geographically and socially isolated people is the development of Internet-based treatments. These programmes combine CBT self-help manuals with Internet technology. Interested people participate in a web-based assessment process that helps to diagnose their primary problems. If they are suitable for SAD treatment, modules providing information and treatment activities are sent to them by email. The participant completes the forms and activities and returns them to the programme, where trained therapists review and provide feedback and suggestions. When one step is completed, another module is sent. Although a recent development, several studies indicate that web-based CBT programmes can produce significant reductions in social anxiety when delivered by trained therapists. One problem with these programmes is that, as with self-help manuals, people can drop out before treatment is finished.

Several programmes have combined web-based treatments with brief telephone contact with therapists and found that the combination increased the completion rate by more than thirty per cent. With adequate technology and knowledge of English, participants can access these programmes from anywhere in the world. The initial success of such programmes may eventually provide treatment for severely avoidant people and get them to the point where they can participate in more direct forms of treatment. At present, only a few such programmes are available.

The Internet is also a source of a vast amount of information. There are very many websites devoted to shyness, blushing problems, social anxiety, and social anxiety disorder. It is valuable to have all this information at the click of a mouse. The user has to take care in identifying the source of the information. Many sites are developed by researchers into social anxiety in universities and clinics; others are set up by charitable organizations and self-help groups devoted to helping people with social anxiety. Nevertheless, just about anyone can set up a website and call themselves whatever they like. However anxious you are, you should exercise extreme caution before giving out personal or financial information about yourself. Reputable organizations can readily be checked out and give you the information to enable you to do this.

## How do I choose a treatment approach?

If you decide that you want treatment, the next step is to learn what options are available in your geographical area. The best approach is to contact your doctor (general practitioner or GP) for advice. Your GP can arrange access to primary care mental health services available through the National Health Service (NHS). Primary care mental health teams work with patients suffering from anxiety, panic attacks, and phobias. The team can include clinical psychologists and counsellors and can provide cognitive behaviour therapy. NHS Direct may also be able to provide advice about what is available in your area. Another way to get this information is to contact professional organizations or anxiety programmes by Internet or telephone. There are several organizations and websites devoted to anxiety or specifically to social anxiety disorder.

One such organization is Social Anxiety UK (SA-UK; you can find details of websites of these organizations in the appendix at the end of the book). SA-UK is an established voluntary organization that was set up in 2000 by individuals who themselves suffered from social anxiety. It is run by volunteers and makes no charge for its services. Their website provides access to information about social anxiety disorder and briefly outlines the various treatments available in the UK. It includes chat rooms and discussion boards. It gives contact information about self-help and support group meetings that are held across the UK. (Currently some thirty-eight groups hold meetings which take place in all four countries of the UK.) Some of these groups have their own website.

Anxiety UK is a charitable organization; its website also gives information about social anxiety disorder and its treatment. It also provides contact details of meetings of self-help groups. The Society has its own team of volunteer practitioners who can provide interventions including cognitive behaviour therapy, counselling and psychotherapy as well as complementary interventions such as hypnotherapy and Neuro-Linguistic Programming. There is a charge for these therapies but the rates for members are reduced and cheaper than the rates normally charged in private practice.

No Panic is a voluntary charity which offers support for those suffering from social anxiety disorder as well as a range of anxiety problems including panic attacks, general anxiety disorder and phobias. As well as a website it provides a telephone helpline (see website for details) where you can speak in confidence to trained volunteers between 10am and 10pm every day and a night helpline for the remainder of the twenty-four-hour period. It offers telephone and written 'recovery' programmes, which are free courses based on cognitive behaviour therapy techniques for people who are not in a position to join groups. The telephone programme involves a group and facilitator who are in contact with one another by means of teleconferencing; the programme involves fourteen weekly one-hour sessions. No Panic Ireland can also be accessed through this website. It offers a telephone helpline for twenty-four hours a week for people in Ireland.

The website of the Anxiety Disorders Association of America (ADAA) provides information about therapists in various countries who have experience in treating social anxiety disorder. Some American clinics offer free or reduced cost treatment for participation in clinical research studies; for example, the Social Anxiety Research Clinic of the Anxiety Disorders Clinic located at the New York State Psychiatric Institute at Columbia University Medical Center, New York and the Adult Anxiety Clinic of Temple University, Pennsylvania.

Other resources include professional psychological associations, such as the British Psychological Society and the Association for Behavioural and Cognitive Therapy in North America. These organizations have websites that provide guidance for people seeking treatment. The British Psychological Society's website maintains a register of psychologists who specialize in psychotherapy. All the psychologists on the register are Chartered Psychologists who are required to be appropriately qualified and who are committed to update their training and professional development. Complaints and disciplinary procedures are available to patients or clients who are dissatisfied with the conduct of the psychologist. The website has a section, 'Find a Psychologist', which permits search by region. The register does give information about the qualifications and specialisms of psychologists who offer therapy including cognitive behaviour therapy.

The British Association for Behavioural and Cognitive Psychotherapy (BABCP) maintains a database of practising BABCP-accredited therapists on its website. This can be searched by region, name of therapist, therapist's areas of specialism, methodologies, and for therapists who speak languages other than English. The database does not include practising therapists who are not accredited by the BABCP. Complaints and disciplinary procedures are available to patients or clients who are dissatisfied with the conduct of the therapist.

It is important to keep your own doctor informed about the steps that you plan to take. Your GP will know your medical history including any medications that you have taken in the past, or are currently taking. He or she may be able to give you advice and may be in a position to refer you to a local mental health centre, primary care mental health services, or clinical psychology department. In addition it would be important to keep your GP informed of any treatment that you are following.

Once you learn what options are available where you live, you will need to consider your own situation. It is important to decide how much time you are willing to devote to treatment and whether you are motivated to attend weekly treatment sessions and complete between-session exercises. The treatment option you select also depends on how you view your social anxiety. If you believe that your social anxiety is primarily physiological, then you may want to begin with a pharmacological intervention. If you feel that your behaviour and thinking patterns contribute to your difficulties, then a psychological treatment approach may be the first step. The National Centre for Health and Clinical Excellence (NICE) produces guidelines on treatments for a range of disorders including depression and anxiety. It has not yet published guidelines on social anxiety disorder. We discuss these guidelines further in chapter 9: see Box 1 in that chapter.

If one approach does not work, you can try the other treatment approach. It is important, however, not to give up on one approach too soon. Significant benefit can require six to twelve months of concerted effort. Pharmacological and psychosocial treatments are often used in combination. Little scientific information is available on the effects of combining the two approaches. The information that is available suggests that combining medication with CBT does not impede treatment effects; however, it is not clear whether the combination results in greater benefit than either approach alone.

## Group versus individual treatment

Some settings offer both group and individual treatment options. Group treatment programmes offer the opportunity to talk about one's experiences with other people who have similar fears. Group members can encourage and support each other. People with SAD are surprised and pleased to learn that others have similar problems and are encouraged by group discussions. Socially anxious people often feel uncomfortable in the first few sessions. Over time, however, anxiety usually fades and group members develop an attachment to each other that allows them to talk more freely. Group participation can be therapeutic in and of itself as it offers a safe place to try out new ways of thinking and behaving. Because group treatment is cost effective, this format is widely used.

Individual treatment offers the advantage of tailoring treatment goals and strategies to the person's individual situation. It also allows more intensive treatment. Individual therapy is particularly useful for people who are extremely anxious about talking in groups or who have complicated life situations or co-existing problems. On average, individual treatment has been found to be somewhat more beneficial than group treatment, most likely because of the greater flexibility and intense focus on the person's specific situation.

## Other problems

### Alcohol reliance

As we noted earlier, as many as twenty per cent of people with SAD rely on alcohol to manage their anxiety. Unfortunately, substance reliance can create additional problems and interfere with standard treatments. If you are socially anxious and also think that your alcohol or drug use is excessive, you will want to seek treatment that can address both problems simultaneously. Individual treatment by a therapist who has experience treating both substance-related problems and anxiety disorders is often the best option.

### Case 4

Ian had been shy as a child and tended to socialize only with his family. After high school, he began his first job as a schedule organizer for a transportation company. The office staff often went for drinks after work, and Ian tried to join them. He found that he felt more relaxed and better able to talk after several beers. He soon began to have a drink or two before going to any social event. Over time, those two drinks increased to four or five, and he was usually somewhat high before going out. On several occasions, he became verbally aggressive, and was even asked to leave one bar after insulting another customer. He began to drink alone at home in the evening in order to stop thinking about his behaviour and the fact that his life was drifting. Unfortunately, drinking resulted in hangovers, and he began to miss work, claiming that he was 'sick'. He sought treatment for SAD but his drinking interfered with his attendance at sessions and between-session exercises. After several months of no progress, his therapist referred him to an alcohol counselling centre.

## Depression

As we discussed earlier, people with SAD often have low mood. Approximately one in four people with SAD is significantly depressed. Research suggests that for most people, depression does not interfere with SAD treatment. In fact, treatment for SAD alone has been shown to alleviate mild to moderate levels of depression. If, however, depression interferes with the person's ability to attend treatment or to apply treatment exercises between sessions, it may be necessary to focus on the lack of motivation that can accompany depressed mood. In this situation, treatment strategies for depression may be incorporated into therapy. One particularly beneficial technique is *behavioural activation*, a strategy that focuses on increasing the person's general activity level. Depressed people often develop the belief that their mood must improve before they can change. In fact, scientific research indicates that increased activity produces mood improvement. This is what behavioural activation seeks to accomplish. There are also cognitive and interpersonal treatment strategies that can help to reduce depression. If depression is a major problem for you and you find yourself unmotivated to change, you may want to seek individual treatment that will address both SAD and depression.

## Panic attacks

Some people with SAD experience panic attacks in social situations. A panic attack is marked by a sudden rush of fear-related physical sensations. Examples include a sudden increase in heart rate, difficulty breathing, shakiness, sweating or chills, nausea, and thoughts that one will pass out or lose control. If panic attacks are confined to social events and are relatively mild, standard SAD treatment will often correct the problem. If panic attacks are severe, occur in other situations, or come out of the blue, treatment strategies specifically designed for panic disorder may be helpful. Panic treatments focus on increasing awareness of the nature of panic attacks; for example, that they are harmless and transient, and on changing inaccurate and exaggerated beliefs about the implications of the attacks. CBT treatment programmes for panic are very effective. Research indicates that more than eighty per cent of people with panic attacks who attend these programmes show significant improvement. If unexpected panic attacks are a problem, it may be useful for you to complete a short-term panic treatment programme prior to beginning treatment for SAD or to combine the two treatments.

Case 5

> Mary was a middle-aged woman who had always had some social anxiety. Her social anxiety became worse following a divorce, and she began to experience panic attacks in group situations. She found parties particularly distressing because she believed that others would think less of her for coming alone. Although she enrolled in a SAD treatment group, she was unwilling to expose herself to group gatherings as suggested by her therapist because she found her panic symptoms to be too distressing. Her therapist then suggested that she take part in a panic disorder programme before tackling her social anxiety.

## How do I find the right therapist?

Two factors are crucial when selecting a psychotherapist.

### Appropriate training

The first is that the therapist has had supervised training in scientifically validated treatments for SAD. Some therapists have developed their own treatments for SAD or use approaches that have never been evaluated. It is usually better to get treatment from a therapist who uses an approach that has been demonstrated to work. Ask the therapist about their treatment approach and either read about it on the web or ask other knowledgeable people to be sure that you are getting an effective treatment. Some therapists try to teach themselves from books or short-term workshops on SAD. This training can be sufficient if the therapist has a good background in CBT or a high level of general skill. When in doubt, however, look for an expert. As discussed earlier, professional organizations and anxiety disorder resource centres can often point you towards expert therapists in your geographical area. Always ask any therapist about their training and experience treating SAD. Competent professionals will be happy to describe their training and experience. Indeed, willingness to describe one's training and to answer questions before treatment begins is required conduct for therapists who are accredited by professional bodies. If the therapist is reluctant to talk about their training, go on to the next person.

## Your personal reaction

The second crucial factor when selecting a therapist is your personal comfort with the person. Even an experienced, distinguished therapist is not a good fit if you do not feel secure with them. This can be difficult for people with SAD to judge because they feel anxious around any professional, particularly when they first meet. One solution to this problem is for you to contract for a few (four to six) sessions, with the agreement that treatment will be re-evaluated after this point. If you continue to feel uncomfortable, discuss this with your therapist and see if that helps. If not, ask for suggestions for other therapists or treatment approaches. Any competent professional will be willing to talk about patients' reservations and make suggestions for other therapists when patient discomfort does not go down over time. Although socially anxious people may continue to feel anxious in treatment sessions for a number of months, you should have some level of trust in your therapist's concern and understanding. Avoid therapists who are unwilling to discuss such matters or encourage you to continue with them if you do not feel treatment is productive. Once again, we encourage you to contact the self-help and professional organizations listed above to find the right therapist for you.

## Key points

- People with SAD often need to decide for themselves whether to seek treatment.
- Treatment can be useful if social anxiety causes impairment in social relationships, school or work performance, leisure activities, ability to handle routine activities of daily living, or health.
- Even if social anxiety does not impair one's performance or ability to function in life, experiencing extreme discomfort during social events can indicate that treatment would be useful.
- A general lack of life satisfaction and an absence of pleasure and happiness can also be signs that one would benefit from treatment.
- There are effective psychological and pharmacological treatments for SAD.
- The most widely studied psychological treatment programmes are based on cognitive behavioural therapy. A number of scientific studies support the effectiveness of these treatments.
- Self-help books and Internet-based treatments can be useful for people with SAD if they are motivated to complete the treatment activities presented.
- Contact with professional organizations or anxiety disorder groups can help to identify treatment resources in your geographical area.

- The first factor to consider when choosing a therapist is whether he or she has experience and expertise with treatments that have been shown to be effective with SAD.
- The second factor to consider is whether you have a general sense of trust in the person's concern and understanding of your situation.
- If one approach to treatment is not working, do not hesitate to try another treatment programme or therapist.

# 7

# Psychological therapy

## What is cognitive behaviour therapy?

As we discussed in chapter 6, the most widely used psychological treatment for social anxiety disorder (SAD) is cognitive behaviour therapy (CBT). In this chapter and in chapter 8 we look at CBT change strategies in greater detail. The primary goal of this approach is to change the factors that *maintain* social anxiety in the present. CBT places particular emphasis on cognitive processes, that is, the way that socially anxious people think about themselves and social events. With this in mind, we begin our discussion of treatment by examining what we know about how thinking helps to maintain social anxiety. This information, which comes from research and clinical observation, will help us understand how CBT works.

### The importance of what we think

The term *cognitive* refers to mental activity, or thinking. CBT looks at two aspects of thinking. The first is thought *content*, that is, what we think about. For example, we can think about pleasant or unpleasant topics; we can think about the past, the present or the future; we can think about ourselves or other people, and so on. Socially anxious people tend to think about topics that maintain their anxiety. Before social events, they may think about past events that did not go well. After social events, they may go over and over what happened and focus on negative aspects of the situation. In CBT, therapists help people reduce the amount of time that they spend thinking about negative topics.

CBT also looks at the *process* of thinking, that is, how we think and the way that we arrive at judgements and conclusions about social events. Arriving at judgements is a complicated process in which the mind has to weigh up different pieces of information. For social events, this includes information about the external situation, such as who is present and how they behave. It also includes information about internal experiences, such as emotional states. Not all types of information are treated equally. Our minds are biologically programmed to give more weight to certain types of information. External cues that signal danger tend to attract our attention and to greatly influence our judgements about events. Negative emotions also strongly affect our judgements. When we feel bad, our thinking and our judgements become more negative, even when, on an objective level, there is little to be negative about. With CBT, people are helped to look at both what they think about and the way that they arrive at their judgements and conclusions about events. In particular, they are taught to understand how negative emotions can distort their thinking so that their judgements about social events are inaccurate, or *biased*. As we will see, *biased judgements* play an important role in maintaining social anxiety.

Thinking occurs on different levels of awareness. We are most familiar with our *conscious* thoughts; however, some thoughts occur outside our awareness. These are referred to as *automatic* thoughts because they occur without conscious

## Case 1

> As a child, one of our patients was cruelly teased by a group of children who made her the topic of their jokes. In her adult life, she was prone to view even friendly joking as a sign that people were making fun of her. On one occasion, an attractive co-worker asked her to come to the gym with him in a somewhat teasing manner. She interpreted his comment to mean that he saw her as flabby and unattractive, whereas it was clear to others that he was trying to ask her out. Here, her past experiences resulted in an automatic judgement that was incorrect. In treatment, she was asked to keep track of situations in which she felt others were making fun of her. After observing a number of similar situations, she began to realize that she was too quick to jump to the conclusion that people were being cruel to her.

control. Automatic thinking can be helpful because it increases mental efficiency. For example, when we encounter friends, we do not have to deliberate about who they are or what they like. Our mind automatically recognizes them and brings up information from past encounters. At times, however, automatic thinking leads to inaccurate judgements. Our mind can jump to illogical conclusions based on previous experiences rather than the current situation. Because automatic thinking occurs rapidly and without conscious control, these judgements can be difficult to recognize and correct. CBT helps people with SAD to become aware of automatic thinking so that their views of current social situations become more accurate (see Case 1).

Research shows that people with social anxiety disorder are prone to a variety of negative cognitions:

- **Negative self-beliefs.** First, they have negative beliefs about themselves. A belief is a general assumption about the world. People with SAD often believe that they are uninteresting, inadequate, or not worthwhile.

- **Negative social beliefs.** They can also have negative social beliefs. For example, they may believe that others are quick to evaluate and to criticize. Some of these beliefs are based on past social experiences. People with SAD are more likely than non-anxious people to report negative childhood experiences, either with their families or in school. These experiences include such events as having shy, overprotective, or critical parents or being the target of rejection, exclusion or bullying in school. As in the example above, when repeated over time, these experiences can lead to negative beliefs that bias judgements about other people.

- **Negative beliefs about anxiety.** Some negative beliefs are based on the presence of social anxiety itself. Socially anxious people are painfully aware of their anxiety and recognize that they experience more anxiety than other people. They can interpret this heightened anxiety to mean that something is wrong with them or that they are in some way defective and different from other people. They may come to believe that showing any sign of anxiety is socially embarrassing and unacceptable because it reveals this 'defect' to others.

- **Negative social predictions.** In addition to negative beliefs, socially anxious people have negative expectations about social events. In CBT, such expectations are referred to as *predictions* because the person is predicting a future outcome. Even before they go into a situation, people with SAD predict that something negative will happen – that they won't handle the situation well or that others will not like them. Interestingly, research shows that these predictions are often overly negative. People with SAD have been found to overestimate the *likelihood* of negative outcomes. In many cases, their negative predictions do not come true. In addition, they overestimate the emotional *cost* of those outcomes, that is, how bad they would feel if something negative actually happened. It is seldom as bad as they expect.

## Case 2

> Edward was concerned that anxiety might cause his hands to shake. He believed that other people would interpret any trembling to mean that he had a neurological disorder and they would then avoid him. He would try to avoid situations in which he felt his hands would be visible. For example, he would not get coffee at the coffee stand because he predicted that his hands would shake and he would spill his coffee, which would cause other people to laugh at him. He was also reluctant to pay for purchases because he predicted that he would spill his money thereby eliciting scorn from the sales assistant. Even though both types of situations involved strangers whom he was unlikely to encounter again, he predicted that he would feel terrible if those outcomes were to happen.

The tendency to make negative predictions leads to social anxiety and avoidance.

- **Negative social interpretations.** People with SAD have been shown to make negative judgements *during* social events. For example, they might interpret a pause in the conversation to mean that the other person is bored. If they stumble over their words or hesitate slightly when talking, they may decide that the other people now view them as odd. As with predictions, these interpretations tend to be exaggerated and overly negative. In fact, people generally do not notice small signs of discomfort or awkwardness, in part because everyone displays such signs at times. If you want to see an example of this, observe the news announcer the next time you watch a live TV news show. You will see that they too occasionally stumble, pause, and mispronounce words despite being paid handsomely for their efforts. The universal tendency to stumble or mispronounce words is why TV shows and movies require multiple takes. People with SAD, however, focus on these small dysfluencies and over-interpret their significance.

- **Biased judgements.** Research shows that people with SAD also tend to *discount* the effectiveness of their own social behaviour, that is, when compared with objective observers, they underestimate their social performance. They also tend to underestimate others' responses to them, for example, how much other people like them. Such negatively biased judgements contribute to social anxiety during social situations. In addition, socially anxious people can decide that an event did not go well even in the absence of objective evidence to support that conclusion.

- **Rumination.** Finally, socially anxious people are prone to *ruminate* after social interactions. By *ruminate* we mean that they go over and over the situation in their mind. They are haunted by the sense that they looked anxious and handled the situation badly. They berate themselves and generally feel bad, often for no reason. Rumination of this sort, like any type of rehearsal, consolidates the memory of the event firmly in mind. Because the person's interpretation often contains an element of distortion, the event can be remembered as more negative than it was.

All of these cognitive factors, negative beliefs, and predictions prior to social events, negative judgements during events, and rumination after events contribute to social anxiety. The major goals of CBT are to identify and correct these negative biases in predictions and judgements, and to reduce post-event rumination. We will discuss this further in chapter 8.

## The importance of what we do (the role of behaviour in social anxiety)

CBT also focuses on the role of behaviour in maintaining social anxiety. In CBT, dysfunctional social behaviour is viewed as an understandable reaction to the negative thinking described above. If you expect social events to have painful negative consequences, it makes sense to take steps to protect yourself. Whereas non-anxious people approach social events with positive goals, such as getting to know other people and enjoying the opportunity to converse, people with SAD report that their goal is self-protection. As a result, they adopt behaviours aimed at increasing their sense of security. These actions are called *self-protective behaviours* or *safety behaviours*.

CBT research shows that socially anxious people use many types of safety behaviours:

- **Avoidance.** The most common safety behaviours are actions designed to avoid attention, such as not talking, avoiding eye contact, and not expressing personal opinions. Here the person tries to prevent rejection or criticism by erasing their own identity. The most toxic use of avoidance as a safety behaviour is when people decide not to even enter a social event. As we've discussed, some socially anxious people avoid nearly all social situations. Broad avoidance of this type offers the temporary benefit of reducing anxiety; however, it also leads to social isolation, loneliness, depression, and makes social anxiety worse.

- **Over-rehearsal.** Another common safety strategy is over-rehearsal, where the person plans and practises everything that they will say during an event. Although rehearsal can be a useful strategy in some situations, such as when preparing to give a speech or to introduce a speaker, some people plan out what they will say before nearly every social gathering. Their social behaviour can then come across as scripted and artificial. Even during interactions, socially anxious people may go over their next comment in their mind while the other person is talking. The downside of this of course, is that they are distracted from what others are saying and may end up saying things that do not fit into the conversation.

## Case 3

> Nora was a music teacher who provided lessons to children. Her father had been a controlling man with a bad temper who would yell at her if he believed she was being 'insolent'. To protect herself, she learned to behave in a pleasant, overly agreeable manner so as to avoid irritating him. She came to believe that she had to maintain a facial expression of pleasant interest and never disagree or people would see her as an unpleasant person and become angry. She felt compelled to nod and smile frequently while others talked. The end result of her agreeable façade was that clients would schedule lessons at inconvenient times and pupils would not listen and follow her instructions. Despite the fact that she was an excellent teacher and well liked, she felt increasingly socially anxious, helpless, and that her life was not under her control.

- **Over-agreeableness.** As can be seen in Case 3, agreeableness can also be used as a safety behaviour. Some people believe that they must always agree with what others say, nod and smile frequently, and maintain an intensely friendly expression to prevent others from disliking them. Social psychologists refer to this pattern as *innocuous sociability*. What distinguishes innocuous sociability from genuine sociability is that the person feels compelled to display this behaviour and does so out of fear of rejection rather than genuine interest.
- **Pretending to be irritable or disinterested.** Some people with SAD use irritability and anger as safety behaviours. The reasoning that underlies this strategy seems to be to reject others before they reject you. Another self-protective strategy is to act aloof or disinterested in others. These behaviours are often used by people who fear that others might pity them. To protect against a loss of pride, they act as though they do not care whether others like them or not. Irritability and disinterest have quite a toxic effect on social relationships. Typically others will draw back when faced with these behaviours.

## Case 4

Anthony was the youngest of four brothers. His older brothers would hit and make fun of him. When he became a teenager, he learned to fight back. As part of this pattern, whenever he felt threatened, he learned to look angry to forestall an attack. As an adult, whenever he entered a situation with unfamiliar people, he would look stern, forbidding, and even angry. Because he was a large man, the end result was that people were somewhat afraid of him and went out of their way not to talk to him. By this time, the safety behaviour was so ingrained that Anthony was not aware of the extent of his unfriendly appearance and simply concluded that other people did not like him.

What may be clear from the discussion above is that safety behaviours often backfire. If we do not talk or maintain eye contact, and seldom express personal views on topics, then we are likely to be overlooked during social events. We may also come across as uninteresting, even boring, which is exactly what the socially anxious person fears. In addition to influencing how other people view us, safety behaviours have been shown to maintain social anxiety. Going to considerable effort to avoid negative outcomes keeps our minds focused on potential danger. The self observation and control required to produce safety behaviours also tend to heighten our tension and fear. A key aspect of CBT is to help people with SAD recognize the toxic effects of safety behaviours and to reduce them as much as possible.

What is unique about CBT is that the behaviour of socially anxious people is viewed as strategic, or designed to meet a goal, namely self-protection. The CBT perspective can be contrasted with social skill theories, which view awkward social behaviour as arising from not having learned what to do. CBT can also be contrasted with psychodynamic views in which behaviour is seen as an expression of an unconscious underlying conflict. According to CBT, people can readily recognize their self-protective concerns and reduce their reliance on safety behaviours without having to learn new behaviour or understand underlying conflicts. We will learn more about this in chapter 8.

## Putting it all together

CBT programmes are based on a *model* of social anxiety disorder that summarizes how the cognitive and behavioural factors described above interact to maintain anxiety. This model divides these factors into three time points, those that occur before, during, and after social events:

- **Before social events.** Social anxiety arises in part from people's negative beliefs about themselves and how other people will respond to them. As noted above, such beliefs are often developed from past negative experiences. People may not even be aware of their underlying beliefs. When they approach a social situation, however, they find that they feel apprehensive and have a sense that something bad is going to happen. We call this *anticipatory anxiety*. Anticipatory anxiety leads to negative expectations, or *predictions*, about what will happen during the social situation, that is the most likely outcome. Together, anticipatory anxiety and negative predictions mean that socially anxious people enter social events already anxious and expecting the worst.
- **During social events.** Anticipatory anxiety has several effects on the person during social events. First, it increases self-consciousness, or self-focused attention. One of the basic biological functions of anxiety is to alert an organism to potential threat so that danger can be avoided. This means that when we experience anxiety, we pay attention to it. Research indicates that focusing on an emotional state actually amplifies it. When we focus on the physical sensations that accompany anticipatory anxiety, our awareness of those sensations is heightened, which further increases

anxiety and the sense of impending danger. Negative predictions also contribute to self-focused attention. Because socially anxious people expect negative outcomes, they carefully monitor and try to control their behaviour so as not to do anything wrong. Unfortunately, by focusing on themselves, they can miss important aspects of the social event, such as other people's comments, which can interfere with their ability to respond effectively.

Anticipatory anxiety and negative predictions lead to *safety behaviours*, strategic actions taken to prevent the feared outcomes from happening and to increase the person's sense of security. It stands to reason that if you expect something bad to happen, you try to prevent it. However, relying on safety behaviours has been shown to increase perceived danger and thereby heighten anxiety. As we noted above, reliance on safety behaviours actually increases the likelihood of negative social outcomes. Not talking or looking at other people can hinder social interactions, which in turn increases anxiety in the situation. Together, self-focused attention and safety behaviours lead socially anxious people to draw overly negative conclusions about events. Because they are so aware of their anxiety and small dysfluencies in their behaviour, they may conclude that the situation went worse than it actually did.

- **After social events.** Socially anxious people tend to engage in repetitive negative thinking, or *rumination*. Rumination involves going over and over events without being able to let them go. Because socially anxious people's social judgements are biased, rumination may centre on an overly negative view of the event. Unfortunately, rumination establishes the negative memory more firmly in mind.

To summarize: negative beliefs and predictions before social events lead to self-focused attention, safety behaviours, and biased judgements during events, and rumination after events that fixes a negative version of the event in memory. These factors operate in a self-perpetuating cycle to maintain the person's original negative beliefs and social anxiety.

Now that we have outlined how cognitive and behavioural processes maintain social anxiety, we will discuss how this information is applied in treatment. We begin with a brief review of the format and central components of CBT. Then, for the remainder of this chapter, we will describe the first of these components. The remaining components will be discussed in detail in chapter 8.

## Treatment format

CBT follows a structured format in which specific activities, or *techniques*, are used to change the cognitive and behavioural processes described above. Therapists first describe the techniques and then help you to apply them to your own situation. Treatment strategies are presented in a stepwise fashion with each exercise building on the previous one. CBT emphasizes doing (taking action) as opposed to talking. The structured, action-oriented treatment format can be contrasted with traditional forms of counselling or therapy, which tend to be open-ended and involve more discourse. Another key element of CBT is the use of between-session activities that help you apply what you have learned in treatment sessions to your daily life. To overcome social anxiety, you must change your behaviour in everyday situations. The inclusion of between-session exercises reflects the CBT emphasis on doing rather than simply talking about social anxiety.

## Components of treatment

Treatment for social anxiety disorder can be broken into several distinct components, each of which has a specific objective:

- The first component focuses on increasing your understanding of social anxiety in general and your own social anxiety in particular. This part of treatment emphasizes identifying your social predictions, judgements, and safety behaviours.
- The second treatment component uses *behavioural experiments* to test the accuracy of negative predictions, judgements, and beliefs. Here, you are asked to deliberately alter your behaviour and observe the outcome.
- A third treatment component is based on the idea of graduated exposure. You are encouraged to expand your participation in social activities, moving from less anxiety-provoking situations and behaviours to more anxiety-provoking ones.
- Finally, some CBT programmes include activities that help you develop closer social relationships. This last component is particularly useful for people with Generalized SAD, who often have difficulty being open with others and developing friendships.

### Component one: developing a personalized understanding of social anxiety disorder

Let's consider what would happen if you were in a CBT programme. The first step in treatment would be to develop a detailed understanding of the nature of your social anxiety. To begin, therapists would describe the model of social anxiety that underlies the CBT approach. Therapists often draw a diagram on a blackboard or pass out sheets that depict the model presented above. Different therapists provide somewhat different models, but the goal is the same – to provide a framework that you can use to understand your own social anxiety. One example of a CBT model of social anxiety is presented in Figure 7.1. This description also introduces important concepts and terminology that will be used in treatment. The therapist will encourage you to discuss how the various aspects of the model

Figure 7.1

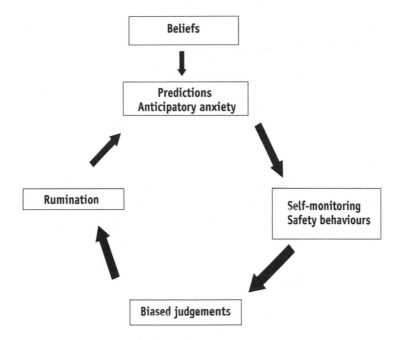

apply to your own situation. The end result of this process is to provide sufficient detail about social anxiety disorder to demystify it, that is, to help you see how your anxiety is the result of an understandable chain of cognitive and behavioural processes, not simply the way you are.

### Component two: self-monitoring

The second step in treatment is to help you apply the model to your day-to-day life. It is one thing to understand an abstract model but quite another to understand one's own thinking and behavioural patterns. To extend the model to your life, you will be encouraged to *self-monitor*, that is, systematically observe and record key aspects of your responses to social events. Self-observation provides the information needed for you to implement later treatment strategies. Monitoring forms are used so that very precise information can be collected. Observing one's behaviour is a skill that takes practice. Therefore, self-monitoring begins by having you record only a few pieces of information about each social situation. Typically, you will list situations that produce social anxiety and rate the severity of the anxiety you experienced in each event. You will also be asked to write a brief description of each event so that you can conduct a detailed analysis of when and how social anxiety arises for you.

As treatment progresses, more columns are added to the forms. Thus, you might be asked to consider what factors would make situations better or worse. For example, a person might find that the presence of more people makes the situation worse and the presence of familiar people makes the situation better. You will be asked to write down your most feared outcome in each anxiety-producing situation, that is, the worst possible outcome. The feared outcome is used to help you to identify your predictions for that event. Once identified, you can then determine whether these predictions come true or not.

Three factors are important in self-monitoring. As discussed earlier, anxiety and the self-focused attention that accompanies it interfere with the ability to see yourself accurately. Therefore, you must learn how to take an objective perspective, that is, to observe yourself as though observing another person. The way to do this is to accept the experience of anxiety without fighting it but rather try to view the event as a way to gather information for treatment. You should also try not to judge or berate yourself but rather focus on the fact that you have taken the first step in overcoming your problem.

Second, you will be asked to systematically rate your level of social anxiety. The monitoring forms include a scale of symptom severity, where $0 =$ no anxiety and $100 =$ panic. Although at first it can be difficult to calibrate one's anxiety, with practice, most people learn to do so. Collecting this information allows you to gain a detailed understanding of the situations and factors that evoke social anxiety, that is, the factors that result in more or less fear. Often, socially anxious people begin treatment with a vague sense that they are socially anxious in all situations. They experience a sense of relief to discover that there are situations that go well and where they do not experience anxiety. They may also be unaware of the exact situational factors that affect their level of discomfort. With objective observation and recording, the problem moves from a global sense of fear to a detailed understanding of your own anxiety profile.

Third, self-observation is most effective if you monitor events as they happen, or as close in time to the event as possible. You will be encouraged to carry forms with you and set aside private times during the day to make notes. Monitoring forms are typically small and easily concealed. Therefore, self-observation can be done unobtrusively. At the very least, you should make daily observations about your social anxiety. The longer you wait before recording events the greater the opportunity for the negative biases caused by anxiety to cloud your observations.

Box 1: Example of a self-monitoring form

| Situation Who? What? Where? When? | Anxiety 0–100 (None to Extreme) | Feared outcome What did you fear would happen in this situation? |
|---|---|---|
|  |  |  |

Self-observation is surprisingly difficult. Anyone who has kept a journal, counted calories, or recorded behaviours like smoking knows this. It is not uncommon for people to record for a day or two and stop. It takes time and effort to make notes. People with SAD, like people with any problem they consider embarrassing, often do not want to look at themselves and their difficulties because it makes them feel bad. Nonetheless, it is difficult, if not impossible, to change a problem that you do not understand. CBT in particular uses very precise change strategies that are based on the specific aspects of the person's individual fears, predictions, and situational profiles. Detailed information makes the rest of treatment more effective. Early CBT sessions typically devote time to trouble-shooting problems that arise during self-monitoring and to helping people have the courage to look their difficulties in the face.

## Component three: identifying safety behaviours

The third step in understanding social anxiety is for you to begin to identify your most frequently used safety behaviours. Different therapists use different strategies to accomplish this. Some therapists use videotaped feedback. In this approach, people are videotaped while they act out a problem situation with the therapist or an assistant. In the first take, you are asked to behave as you normally would. You and your therapist then review the tape, and you identify the safety behaviours that you used in that situation. Next, you repeat the situation, this time trying to drop or reduce those safety behaviours. Finally, you compare the two tapes to see first hand how you come across when using and not using safety behaviours. Most people find that they look more comfortable and friendly when they drop their safety strategies. For some individuals, this is a highly beneficial experience in and of itself, in addition to increasing their awareness of their safety behaviours.

Other therapists ask people to complete a questionnaire that lists various safety behaviours and to reflect on which ones they use. The questionnaire can be combined with self-monitoring daily social events. Thus, following each event, you note which safety behaviours you used in that specific situation. This approach has the advantage of extending the idea of safety behaviours to your own life situation and helps to increase your awareness of when and how often you use these behaviours. Another approach that is used in group treatment is to have participants identify the safety behaviours they use in treatment sessions. This approach is helpful for people who are severely avoidant since they may not have many other social events to observe. However it is done, it is important for you to understand the notion of safety behaviours and to recognize what steps you take to try to ward off negative outcomes.

### Component four: develop a personalized model

Throughout the first stage of treatment, you will be encouraged to use the basic CBT model of social anxiety as a framework to make sense of your own experiences. As you monitor your social anxiety, feared outcomes, and identify your safety behaviours, you use what you have learned to develop a personalized version of the model to pinpoint the factors that contribute to social anxiety in your own life. Some therapists provide worksheets that you can use to diagram your most problematic situations. To illustrate this, let's take the case of Anthony described above. You remember that Anthony believed that people were cruel and that he had to protect himself from verbal and even physical attacks. Figure 7.2 depicts a personalized model that describes Anthony's beliefs, predictions, safety behaviours, biased judgements, and post-event thoughts for situations where he encountered unfamiliar people. As you can see, because of his negative beliefs about others, when he entered a social situation he predicted that the other people would be hostile. He therefore used his habitual safety behaviours, which were to look stern or angry, to try to prevent the person from expressing hostility. Although he assumed that his forbidding appearance staved off hostility, in fact his behaviour led others to cut the conversation short and avoid him. Following such events, he was left wondering why people did not seem to like him.

Self-monitoring and completing diagrams clarifies the processes that drive social anxiety for each individual. This information sets the stage for the implementation of treatment strategies aimed at changing those processes. In chapter 8, we

Figure 7.2

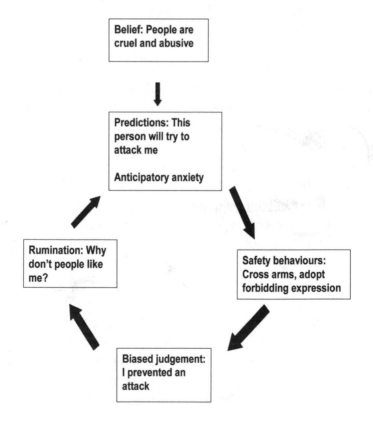

will consider how you can use the information that you have collected to overcome social anxiety.

## Key points

- CBT emphasizes the role of thinking in the maintenance of social anxiety disorder.
- CBT addresses two aspects of thinking: thought content, what the person thinks about; and thought process, how the person arrives at judgements and conclusions about social events.
- Thinking can be conscious or automatic. Automatic thinking occurs rapidly and without full awareness.
- Automatic thinking can lead to problems if it causes people to jump to conclusions based on past experiences rather than present events.
- People with SAD have been found to have several types of negative cognitions, including negative beliefs about themselves and others, negatively biased predictions for social events, inaccurate judgements during social events, and rumination after events.
- Negative beliefs lead to negative predictions and anticipatory anxiety before the person enters a social situation.
- Anticipatory anxiety and negative predictions result in self-focused attention and the use of safety behaviours to ward off the expected negative outcomes.
- Post-situation rumination can fix overly negative interpretations of events in memory.
- Together these cognitive processes can create a cycle of events that maintains social anxiety.
- CBT can be divided into a number of treatment components.
- The first component of CBT is to increase understanding of social anxiety disorder. Therapists do this by presenting a

model that summarizes what is known about social anxiety and encouraging patients to apply this model to their experiences.

- Self-monitoring is an important activity in treatment because it increases patients' awareness of how social anxiety works in their lives. Detailed information is necessary for successful application of CBT strategies.
- Over time, therapists help patients develop a personalized model that describes the cognitive and behavioural processes that contribute to their own social anxiety.

# 8

# Overcoming social anxiety: strategies for change

Chapter 7 described the first step in psychological treatment approaches, which is to develop a detailed understanding of the factors that contribute to your social anxiety. The end result of that process is an individualized model, or summary, that describes how your thinking and behaviour contribute to your social anxiety in specific situations. Although this model will be refined and expanded over time, once key thought patterns and safety behaviours are identified, you can begin to take steps to overcome your social fears.

A number of strategies have been found to be useful in reducing social anxiety. These strategies are focused on the cognitive and behavioural processes that maintain anxiety. An important advance in CBT has been to use behavioural exercises to evaluate the accuracy of the negative thinking that triggers social anxiety. Let's consider some of the CBT strategies.

## Strategies for change

### Evaluating safety behaviours

As we discussed in chapter 7, people with SAD often use *safety behaviours* to prevent negative social outcomes. Safety behaviours can be useful if indeed something negative is likely to happen. For example, if you work with an angry, critical supervisor, it may be necessary to be cautious in what you say and do, and try to deflect attention. At times, however, socially anxious people rely on safety behaviours when they are not necessary. In this case, these behaviours cause problems because they maintain a sense of danger and fear, lead to self-focused attention, and interfere with interactions with others. For example, if the supervisor described above is trying to provide you with helpful feedback, avoiding him or not talking openly about the problem may prevent you from improving your work performance. It may even convey the impression that you do not care about the job. Eliminating unnecessary safety behaviours has been shown to reduce fears of all types, and this is an important goal in treatment. In CBT, you are asked not to prejudge the effects of your typical safety behaviours. Instead, you are encouraged to take a questioning approach and test for yourself whether safety behaviours are useful or actually help to perpetuate your fear.

The most effective way to evaluate the usefulness of safety behaviours is with *behavioural experiments*. A behavioural experiment involves several steps:

1. To begin, you target a specific situation which produces social anxiety.
2. Then, you identify your prediction about what will happen in the situation, the negative outcome that you fear will occur. For example, a person may predict that they will

completely freeze up, which will cause others to stare at them or back off.

3. The third step is to pinpoint the safety behaviours that you use to prevent that negative outcome. The person in our example may do such things as try not to talk much and always nod and agree because he or she believes these actions will prevent disapproval.

4. The fourth step in the experiment is to reduce those safety behaviours and observe what happens. For example, the person may talk more and see what happens. Does he freeze up? If so, how do others respond? When observing the outcome of the experiment, it is important that you take an objective stance. Look at the situation as an outside observer would and look for objective evidence as to what happened. Did people frown, stop talking, and withdraw from the conversation? Or did their behaviour remain the same?

5. The final step in this process is to enter similar situations a number of times, alternating between using and dropping safety behaviours. Thus, on one occasion, you should behave as you usually do; on the next occasion you should try to eliminate your safety behaviours. Then compare the outcomes of the two approaches. Ask yourself two questions: in each situation, 'how did I feel?' and 'what was the social response?' By comparing the two situations, you can decide whether safety behaviours are necessary or just get in the way. More times than not, people find that their safety behaviours are not needed because the feared outcome did not happen. Most people also discover that they feel more genuine ('like I am being myself') and spontaneous when they drop unnecessary safety behaviours.

## Example 1

Elizabeth worked as a sales assistant in a clothes shop. Although the assistants were expected to talk with customers, her social anxiety made it difficult for her to do so. Her prediction was that if she were to talk much, customers would see her as awkward and unintelligent. She identified her safety behaviours as avoiding eye contact, speaking very softly, and confining herself to brief comments such as 'hi'. As an experiment, she decided to alternate between using and not using her safety behaviours. Thus, with the first customer, she would avoid eye contact and try to avoid drawing attention to herself; with the next customer, she maintained longer eye contact, smiled, and asked 'how are you today?' When she compared the outcomes of the two types of events, she noticed that customers were friendlier and more positive to her when she reduced her safety behaviours. She also found that she actually felt more comfortable when she was not focusing on feeling safe.

## Example 2

Jennifer's co-workers often stood around the office coffee machine to discuss current events or their weekend activities. Jennifer was too anxious to join them and would generally hide in her cubicle during these conversations. Her predictions were that anything she might say would be viewed as uninteresting and that her co-workers would slowly walk away were she to talk. As a behavioural experiment, she began to stand with the others. When she noticed that people were friendly to her, she tried making brief observations (for example, about the weather). She noticed that people smiled and talked to her more when she talked than when she did not. Over time, she began to alternate between expressing her opinions one day and simply agreeing with others' comments on the next day. She found that rather than walking away, her co-workers responded to her opinions with interest and talked more to her when she expressed opinions than when she did not. At the end of treatment, she reported that she felt she had made some friends at work. She also felt better about herself.

## Example 3

Marian experienced social anxiety in situations in which others had to wait in line behind her. For example, she became nervous when paying in shops because she believed that others would feel irritated with her because they were being inconvenienced. To evaluate that prediction, she identified a number of specific situations in which she could deliberately inconvenience others. In one experiment, she went to a bakery, made a small purchase while others were waiting behind her, and paid with change. To add to their inconvenience, she counted the change slowly. She observed that most people simply waited patiently. Although several people shifted back and forward on their feet, no one expressed irritation or looked angry. Another experiment was to make right turns while driving, a situation in which she predicted that the drivers behind her would sound their horn and make rude gestures when they had to wait for her. After repeatedly turning right, she found that drivers very seldom sounded their horn and no one shouted or gestured rudely at her. Even when drivers beeped their horn at her, they generally only tapped their horn, and to her surprise, it did not bother her all that much. Over time, Marian became more comfortable with others waiting for her.

### Evaluating the effects of anxiety-related behaviours

Some people with SAD worry about displaying behaviours associated with anxiety. For example, they are afraid that their hands will tremble, that they will awkwardly stumble over words when speaking, or that there will be inordinately long pauses in the conversation. Their prediction is that these behaviours will cause other people to see them as odd or inadequate. The behavioural experiment procedure described above can be used to evaluate whether such fears are accurate, that is, whether these behaviours do cause negative social responses. Here, people are asked to *deliberately* produce the anxiety behaviour and observe the outcome.

## Example 4

When Edward was anxious, his hands would tremble slightly, in part because he tried to keep them absolutely still. His expectation (prediction) was that his trembling would cause him to spill things and others would look at him in a critical manner or laugh at him. As a behavioural experiment, he was asked to go into a coffee shop and deliberately make his hands shake so that he spilled his coffee on his table. He then counted the number of people who looked at him, as well as how many people laughed or gave signs of disapproving of his clumsiness. Much to his surprise, he found that most people did not even notice the spill. Those few who did look up showed no signs of disapproval or disgust. One woman even handed him paper napkins and offered to help mop up the coffee. Edward repeated the experiment in a variety of situations. He spilled food in restaurants, dropped newspapers in the street, and spilled water at work. Again, he found that few people noticed his hands or the spills. Those who did usually tried to help him. Edward concluded that there was no evidence to support his negative predictions.

## Example 5

Allan was generally uncomfortable in group situations. One of his fears (predictions) was that his mind would go blank and there would be a pause in the conversation. He believed that this would make the rest of the group uncomfortable and they would avoid looking at or talking to him. As an experiment, he was asked to pause deliberately and stumble over words. He began with a social situation in which he was dining with friends. He began to talk and then paused for two seconds. He found that his friends did not appear to notice the pause. He moved on to longer pauses with the same outcome. He then tried saying 'ah ... ah' several times while talking. Again, no one seemed to notice. After repeating the experiment by pausing and stumbling over words in other social situations and during group meetings at work, he became less concerned about pauses and stammering. He also found that he took greater pleasure in socializing with his friends when he felt less pressure to prevent pauses.

From these examples, you can see that socially anxious people tend to overestimate the visibility and consequences of anxiety-related behaviours.

## Using observation to evaluate negative social beliefs

As we discussed in chapter 7, socially anxious people often have negative beliefs about themselves and others. A second type of experiment is used to test the accuracy of those beliefs. Here, the person is encouraged to systematically observe social situations to evaluate the belief. Once again, it is important that the person

### Example 6

One of David's core beliefs was that he was not interesting. To try to overcome what he perceived to be a deficiency, he pressured himself to try to tell witty stories. This pressure had the paradoxical effect of increasing his anxiety and making his mind go blank. He compared himself unfavourably to a friend, whom he saw as an accomplished conversationalist who regaled their friends with funny stories. As part of treatment, David was asked to observe his friend to determine whether the friend was always interesting and witty. He surreptitiously kept track of his friend's comments and mentally evaluated how interesting and humorous they were. David found that the majority of his friend's comments were routine small talk and that some of his stories were long winded and not all that funny. He also noticed that other people occasionally acted somewhat bored with his friend's tendency to dominate the conversation. He then observed conversations in a variety of other situations. He kept track of the topics discussed in these situations and calculated what proportion of people's comments were astute, interesting, and funny. He found that most people only used humour occasionally. Interestingly, he also learned that he liked people who did not make jokes but rather were warm and accepting. He recognized that there are qualities that are more important to relationships than entertaining people. As a result of the exercise, David stopped pushing himself to deliver humorous stories.

observes the situation from an objective perspective and l
for clear evidence as to whether the belief is accurate or not

## Example 7

> Peter was an IT specialist who was required to give technical
> talks in organizational settings. He had a number of nega-
> tive beliefs about his professional competence. One specific
> belief was that he did not speak well. He believed that he
> mispronounced words, verbally jumbled his sentences, and
> had to correct what he said more than most people. To eval-
> uate this belief, he decided to observe other people talking
> in professional situations. He attended lectures and kept
> track of the number of times speakers mispronounced or
> stumbled over words. He also listened to talk radio shows
> while driving and counted the number of times the host
> paused, said 'ah', or corrected what he or she had said. Peter
> learned that other speakers also displayed such verbal tics
> and that this did not distract from their message. This infor-
> mation helped him modify his negative view of himself.

## Example 8

> Zoë was a student whose social anxiety caused problems in
> school. Following any occasion on which she spoke in class,
> she would ruminate about what she said. In particular, she
> believed that her teacher and classmates thought her com-
> ments were 'stupid'. As part of treatment, she was asked to
> specify how people would behave if they truly felt she was
> saying foolish things. She decided that they would roll their
> eyes when she spoke, not sit by her in class, and avoid talk-
> ing with her after class. To evaluate her belief, she kept track
> of how her classmates and teacher responded to her on the
> days that followed her attempts to speak in class compared
> with days when she was silent. She learned that her class-
> mates did not roll their eyes and did not avoid her after she
> spoke up. Her teacher actually became friendlier and would
> talk to her about her comments after class. As a result of this
> information, Zoë began to speak more often in class and felt
> more confident about approaching other students.

## Example 9

> Betty was an older woman who had returned to work follow-
> ing a divorce. Because she had been away from the work-
> force, she felt insecure about her ability to handle her job.
> Her self-doubt was heightened by frequent criticism from
> her supervisor. Her belief was that the supervisor's criticism
> was warranted because her performance was so poor. To
> evaluate this belief, she began to observe how the supervi-
> sor responded to other office workers. She discovered that
> the supervisor was also critical of the other three women
> who worked in the office. This knowledge led her to realize
> that the supervisor was simply a critical person and that her
> criticism of Betty was part of a general pattern of negative
> behaviour towards others. As a result of her observations,
> Betty began to make sympathetic comments to the other
> women when the supervisor criticized them. Soon, the four
> women routinely lunched together and provided each other
> with mutual support to offset the effects of an unfriendly
> work environment.

## Evaluating the 'cost' of negative outcomes

People who use the behavioural experiment and observational
exercises described above most frequently discover that social
events go better than they expected and that their predicted
negative outcomes did not happen. Occasionally, however, we
all encounter negative people or negative responses. As in the
cases described above, Betty had to work with a critical supervisor, and Marian occasionally had other drivers sound their
horn at her when she delayed the traffic. Socially anxious
people have a tendency to focus on those negative events and to
exaggerate their significance. Therefore, another important
skill to learn is how to place these events in perspective, that is,
not to let them unduly affect how one feels. In CBT, people are
taught how to objectively evaluate the 'cost' of negative social
outcomes, that is how 'bad' it would be if they did happen, by

rating the extent to which such events affect their lives. For example, although Betty did not like her supervisor, upon reflection she decided that the supervisor did not affect her relationships with her family and friends, and even had the positive effect of helping her connect with her co-workers. By deliberately evaluating the cost, she was able to place her supervisor's behaviour in perspective and to conclude that, while unpleasant, the supervisor did not affect her life very much. Similarly, when Marian rated the cost of being honked at, she decided that it really did not matter to her if strangers honked at her occasionally. Because socially anxious people tend to overemphasize the importance of negative outcomes, learning how to place them in the broader context of one's life is a crucial skill to overcoming social fears. In fact, learning not to overestimate the emotional cost of negative outcomes is a major factor in overcoming social anxiety.

## Approaching social situations

### Expanding social activities

The change strategies described above are first applied to social events that the person routinely encounters. As people adjust their beliefs and predictions to be more accurate, they are encouraged to expand the range of situations they enter. Even small levels of social anxiety can narrow our lives. As anxiety becomes more severe, it can constrict our lives to a narrow routine of attending work and going home. Some people only interact with family members or one or two school friends, or even become completely socially isolated. Social anxiety can also keep us from participating in sports, exercise, and hobbies. When this happens, life becomes monotonous and unsatisfying. To overcome social anxiety, anxious people must gradually expand the range of events in which they participate. It is most effective to do this in a stepwise fashion.

In psychological treatment programmes, people learn how to arrange social events into a hierarchy in terms of how much anxiety they evoke. Each week they are encouraged to enter new situations, beginning with those that produce less anxiety and gradually moving to those that produce greater anxiety. As they do so, they follow the procedure outlined above for conducting behavioural experiments. They write down their predictions for the situation, enter the situation and rate their anxiety and the safety behaviours they use to prevent the feared outcomes. Next, they use either the behavioural experiment procedure or observational exercises to evaluate their predictions and beliefs about that situation.

People whose social anxiety leads to severe avoidance may become anxious when they even contemplate leaving home. It can be useful for avoidant people to begin expanding their lives by simply getting out of the house, walking, and entering situations where there are few people. Increasing participation in non-social activities reduces the fear that arises from leaving home, increases their energy, and improves their mood. Indeed one of the most effective ways to overcome the mild depression that often accompanies social anxiety is to become active. Physical activity is particularly helpful in reducing depression. As avoidant people become more active, they can begin to enter social situations.

Some treatment programmes teach relaxation techniques to help people cope with any feelings of anxiety they experience in unfamiliar situations. A number of techniques have been shown to increase the person's ability to relax. There is disagreement, however, as to whether using such relaxation strategies is useful. Focusing on relaxing can keep people's attention focused on their anxiety and thereby heighten their level of fear. Another concern is that the relaxation technique can become a safety behaviour, and people can come to believe that they must be relaxed before they enter a new situation. Some research suggests that to overcome anxiety, it is better for us to experience anxiety than to try to control it. By experiencing anxiety, we learn that it will decrease if we remain in the situation, particularly if we change our negative thought patterns.

## Developing social relationships

Some people experience social anxiety only in performance situations, such as public speaking and job interviews, or with strangers. These people may feel comfortable with friends, family, partners, and non-evaluative work situations. Therefore, social anxiety does not disrupt their personal relationships. For some of us, however, social anxiety also occurs during social interactions. In this case, social anxiety can inhibit the development of meaningful friendships and romantic relationships, and can even prevent the person from talking openly with family members. As with other types of social anxiety, *social interaction anxiety* often arises from negative beliefs. Examples of such beliefs are 'I don't know what to say', 'I'm boring', 'I'm odd', or have some other personal inadequacy that makes me unlikeable and unworthy of other people's attention. Treatment strategies that focus on relationship development can be useful in addressing such beliefs.

Many socially anxious people believe that they lack the social skills to relate to people. They have the sense that there are unwritten social rules and behaviours for developing relationships that they have not learned. Is this accurate? There is no doubt that some social situations require specialized knowledge and behavioural skill. Take the case of a royal lunch party. Few of us would know the correct protocol and etiquette for such an event. Similarly, when we encounter people from another culture, different social norms can apply and our behaviour may need to be adjusted to be appropriate. Those unusual events aside however, on the whole, research studies indicate that most socially anxious people have the necessary repertoire of behaviours to develop friendships. It is just that negative beliefs and concerns with self-protection prevent them from doing so. Because social anxiety leads to self-focused attention, when we are anxious, we do not consider how our self-protective behaviour affects other people.

CBT therapists encourage people to look at themselves from the perspective of the people with whom they interact. For example, you might ask yourself how self-focused attention and self-preoccupation are likely to be viewed by other people. Upon reflection, most people recognize that self-preoccupation distracts them from fully attending to other people. Others can perceive this lack of attention as a lack of interest in them as a person. Few of us seek to become friends with people who give the appearance of being uninterested in us. Being focused on and attentive to what the other person is saying and doing communicates that you value that person. As a rule, people are interested in those who are interested in them.

It is also useful to consider how safety behaviours are inter-preted by others. Socially anxious people may not realize that their safety behaviours, like all other behaviours, send an inter-personal *message* – it tells the other person what you want them to do. Consider what your behaviour is 'saying' to others. With reflection, most of us can recognize the message we are sending. For example, avoiding eye contact and not talking has been found to 'tell' the other person not to talk to us, or at least that is how others read those behaviours. Similarly, being overly agreeable can come across as artificial. Feigning lack of interest in others or self-protective unfriendliness sends a definite 'I want you to go away' message.

Group treatment is a good context for learning to under-stand your typical interpersonal messages. One group exercise is to have participants use their safety behaviours for part of a session and then drop them for the second part. The other group members then provide feedback on how the change affects their reactions to the person. It is also important for people to reflect on how they feel about others and about themselves when using or not using self-protective behaviour. Usually people feel better about others when they drop their safety strategies. Importantly, they also report that they feel more genuine and less self-conscious, that is, more 'like myself'.

Example 10

> In chapter 7, we described the case of Anthony, who learned to put on an unfriendly or angry expression as a safety behaviour. His prediction was that if he did not look 'strong' and forbidding, others would criticize and bully him. He was extremely anxious around other people and, as a result, had become almost completely socially isolated. Therefore, he decided to conduct his behavioural experiment in the treatment group. For the first part of one session he behaved as he usually did, that is, he maintained a forbidding facial expression. In the second half of the session, he made an effort to keep his expression neutral or even pleasant. When the therapists asked the group members for their reactions, they reported that when he looked forbidding they felt afraid of him, but that when he smiled they liked and felt closer to him. The outcome of this experiment came as a surprise to Anthony, who confided that he felt small and weak inside. It had not occurred to him that his scowl and stern expression frightened others. He began to consider the possibility that he was not unlikeable but rather his behaviour kept other people away.

As we discussed in chapter 7, some CBT programmes use videotaping to help socially anxious people appreciate their interpersonal impact. Here, participants enact problem situations just as they would normally handle them. Then, they observe themselves on tapes and consider how their behaviours come across, that is, how another person would interpret their behaviour. They then repeat the situation, adjusting their behaviour to send the interpersonal message they want to convey. Usually socially anxious people are able to adjust their behaviour spontaneously. When they see themselves and consider the interpersonal impact of their behaviour, they recognize what they need to do in order to more effectively relate to others. In some cases, the socially anxious person may seek advice from the therapist or other group members about how they could modify their behaviour to convey the message they want to convey.

## Understanding basic principles of interpersonal behaviour

Socially anxious people can also lack awareness of the basic principles that underlie social interactions. Researchers have identified several important principles.

### THE RECIPROCITY PRINCIPLE

According to this principle, social behaviour tends to 'pull' for a reciprocal response, that is, a response that matches the other person's behaviour. What you give is what you tend to get back. One important example of this principle is that people tend to reciprocate the emotional tone of others. Thus, when a person is warm, it tends to 'pull' a warm, friendly response from us. When the person's behaviour appears unfriendly and disinterested, we tend to reciprocate with disinterest or aloofness ourselves. The reciprocity principle can readily be applied to safety behaviours as well. As we've seen, self-protective behaviours often convey a lack of interest or a negative reaction towards the other person, even if this is not truly so. In treatment, the reciprocity principle can be tested in behavioural experiments. Socially anxious people are encouraged to try different types of behaviour and look at the response those behaviours pull from others.

## THE LIKING EFFECT

Research indicates that openness, or self-disclosure, is a key factor in developing relationships. Self-disclosure refers to willingness to talk about one's personal experiences, feelings, and opinions. Research has shown that we tend to like people more when they are open and share information about themselves. Social psychologists refer to this as the *liking effect*. A second principle is that reciprocity is important. Thus, if we are talking about intimate feelings and experiences, we prefer people who are equally open in return as opposed to people who give perfunctory, superficial replies. Conversely, when we talk about routine or non-intimate topics, we feel uncomfortable if others respond by revealing deeply personal information. In general then, reciprocity in self-disclosure leads to greater likeability.

Reciprocal self-disclosure has been shown to be a key factor in developing friendships and other close relationships. Friendships develop over time through a process of mutual openness. Most relationships begin with relatively superficial conversation. Then one person opens up a small amount. If the other person reciprocates this openness, the relationship moves to a somewhat deeper level. The first person may then talk about more personal experiences. If the second person reciprocates, over time, the two people will develop a closer relationship. Talking openly increases the mutual trust that is the basis of friendships. Unfortunately, socially anxious people often feel uncomfortable giving their opinions and revealing themselves because they fear that others will find them boring or pitiable. The end result is that they fail to reciprocate other people's self-disclosure, which reduces the other person's liking for them. The relationship does not deepen, and they choke off the potential friendship. This well-established principle should not be taken to imply that you *must* reciprocate other people's openness. You may not like the person. In this case, you can simply not reciprocate the person's openness. This tends to keep the relationship on a less personal level.

## THE SIMILARITY EFFECT

Research shows that we tend to like people we perceive to be similar to ourselves. Perceived similarity has been shown to be influenced by both openness and familiarity. That is, when people are open and talk about themselves, we tend to see them as similar to ourselves and we like them more. In addition, the more frequently we talk to or even just see another person, the more familiar they seem, the more we see them as similar to ourselves, and the more we like them. Thus, to develop closer relationships, it is helpful to seek out people who share similar characteristics and interests with us. According to the attraction-similarity principle, this will increase the likelihood that others will respond positively to us. It is also helpful to become involved in activities where we have ongoing contact with the same people. With repeated contact come feelings of similarity and liking. Finally, socially anxious people tend to focus on dissimilarities instead of characteristics that they share with others. This tendency increases their belief that they are different than others. Therefore, another useful strategy is to deliberately identify and focus on similarities between ourselves and others and draw on those similarities in social interactions.

## What if you *don't* know what to do?

At times, we all encounter unfamiliar social situations that we do not know how to handle. This will happen for socially anxious people as well. The difference is that non-anxious people do not let themselves sink into self-doubt and anxiety. Instead, they seek out information on what is expected and how others handle such events. It can be useful for socially anxious people to learn that not knowing what to do does not mean that they are inadequate but rather a cue that they should gather information.

## Updating beliefs and predictions

The strategies discussed above are most effective when people systematically record the outcomes of behavioural experiments, observational exercises, and relationship-building activities. Monitoring forms and rating scales are useful in helping to overcome negative beliefs and behaviours. Where possible, it is helpful to quantify the results. For example, you may want to count how many times dropping safety behaviours led to a positive outcome and how often it led to a negative outcome. Similarly, you might count how often other people stammer or mispronounce words compared with how often you do so yourself. Using numbers helps us look objectively at our beliefs and expectations to see if they need to be updated.

We generally accept our beliefs and judgements without question. Social beliefs and judgements often arise from automatic thinking, which occurs without our full awareness. To overcome negative thinking, it is important to evaluate periodically whether inaccurate automatic thinking is biasing our interpretation of social events. Negative beliefs about self and others are learned in childhood. Although they may have been accurate in the past, they may now be outdated. Social anxiety, and the resulting self-focused attention and safety behaviours, can prevent us from fully experiencing social situations. As a result, we can miss new and important information that would allow us to revise previously learned beliefs. In CBT, after several months of using the change strategies discussed above, socially anxious people are encouraged to evaluate the evidence for and against their social beliefs. It can be helpful to add up the numbers or list evidence that confirms or disconfirms each belief and prediction. People often find that negative beliefs and expectations no longer apply to current social interactions or may apply only to some, not all, social events. Figure 8.1 presents a form that can be used to update old beliefs and expectations.

Figure 8.1 Updating negative social beliefs

| Belief | Evidence consistent with belief | Evidence not consistent with belief | Modified belief (based on new experiences) |
|---|---|---|---|
|  |  |  |  |
|  |  |  |  |
|  |  |  |  |

## Treatment effectiveness

The strategies for overcoming social anxiety presented in this chapter form the core of cognitive behavioural treatments for social anxiety disorder. People who seek treatment for social anxiety disorder should not simply rely on books or our opinions about their effectiveness. They should ask about the research evidence that supports the effectiveness of any treatment programme they enter. Researchers use treatment outcome studies to evaluate whether treatment works. In the case of CBT, multiple well-controlled treatment outcome studies, including several conducted in the UK, indicate that these strategies significantly reduce social anxiety for the majority of people with SAD. Another important question is whether this improvement is maintained over time. Again, research studies have found that the changes produced by CBT last for years. But, don't just take our word for it – go on the web or to the library and read about these and other studies on social anxiety.

Clinical studies also provide some guidance as to the best way to implement the strategies described in this chapter. First, behavioural experiments and observational exercises must be very specific, that is tailored to the specific situation. Thus, it is important to specify precisely the exact belief or prediction for that situation and to identify the safety behaviours used to prevent negative outcomes in that situation. In addition, people must engage in these activities frequently. There is greater reduction in social anxiety when the activities are conducted each day for one week than when the same number of exercises is spread over several weeks. Finally, it is important that people with SAD continue to apply the strategies for a year or longer following treatment. It takes time to change. Three or four months of treatment is only the beginning of the change process. To completely overcome social anxiety, the strategies must be applied for a significant period of time in every situation in which you experience social anxiety. Furthermore, if social anxiety comes back, you should take out your notes and forms and implement the change strategies again. If you are willing to do so, there is a very good chance that social anxiety will be reduced to the point that it no longer causes distress and life impairment.

## Key points

- Psychological treatment programmes concentrate on the cognitive and behavioural processes that maintain social anxiety.

- In CBT, behavioural exercises are used to evaluate the accuracy of negative beliefs and predictions.
- Behavioural experiments are exercises in which the person changes his or her behaviour and observes the results.
- Behavioural experiments are often used to evaluate whether safety behaviours are helpful or simply maintain anxiety.
- Behavioural experiments in which people deliberately engage in feared behaviours can be used to evaluate whether such behaviours as trembling, pausing, or stammering lead to negative social outcomes.
- Observation experiments can be used to evaluate the accuracy of negative beliefs. Here, the person often collects information about a belief by observing other people.
- A key skill in overcoming social anxiety is learning how to place any negative social outcomes that do occur in a broader perspective.
- As socially anxious people learn how to evaluate their negative thought patterns, they can begin to expand their range of social activities.
- When social anxiety interferes with the development of relationships, it can be useful to reflect on basic principles of interpersonal behaviour.
- An important interpersonal principle is that of reciprocity. People tend to like people who reciprocate their behaviour.
- Friendships and close relationships develop over time through a process of reciprocal self-disclosure.
- After using the change strategies described in this chapter, socially anxious people should update their social beliefs and predictions in light of the evidence.
- People who seek treatment should always ask whether research has shown the treatment approach to be effective.
- The effectiveness of the CBT strategies described here is supported by a number of treatment outcome evaluation studies.

# 9

# Medication

## Medication in the treatment of social anxiety disorder

The emphasis in this book is on psychological forms of treatment for social anxiety disorder. Nevertheless, pharmaceutical medication is an established form of treatment for psychological problems including anxiety disorders, obsessive-compulsive disorder and depression. There has been extensive research into its application to social anxiety disorder. No new forms of pharmaceutical treatment have been developed specifically for social anxiety disorder. The SSRIs (Selective Serotonin Reuptake Inhibitors) have emerged as the treatment of choice for social anxiety disorder, but other types of medication have been used and their effectiveness has been investigated. Because you may have heard about drug treatments for shyness and social anxiety or may be offered this form of treatment by your doctor this chapter provides short descriptions of four pharmaceutical treatments for social anxiety disorder and explains some issues that should be taken into account when considering their use. It discusses the rationale for drug treatment. Why might medication be expected to be effective for the treatment of psychological conditions? This chapter evaluates evidence for the effectiveness of this approach. It also describes limitations on its use.

Two approaches to the treatment of social anxiety disorder involve classes of drugs that were originally used in the treatment of depression, the SSRIs and the MAOIs (monoamine oxidase inhibitors). Another two classes of drugs have been widely applied to the treatment of anxiety disorders, beta blockers and the benzodiazepines. All these drugs are prescription-only. They may be prescribed by the patient's doctor or by a psychiatrist to whom the patient has been referred. As we shall see later in the chapter, drug treatments for social anxiety disorder require patients to work closely with their doctor in the management of treatment. It is important to emphasize that the appropriateness of any drug, the correct dose to be administered, and the management of any side effects and any problems in stopping taking the drug will vary from one patient to another and will require clinical judgement.

## Evaluating pharmaceutical treatments

Before discussing each of these classes of drugs in turn, it is worth asking how we know that medication works in the treatment of social anxiety disorder. Medical treatment draws upon the expertise and clinical experience of doctors who prescribe treatments for their patients and monitor their patients' progress. Drugs are made available to doctors by pharmaceutical companies, which develop new drugs and discover new applications for existing ones. The companies carry out or commission research into the safety and effectiveness of medication including optimal dosage levels. The National Institute for Health and Clinical Excellence (NICE) provides guidance for the National Health Service in England and Wales on the promotion of good health and the prevention and treatment of ill health. This includes making recommendations about the effectiveness and safety of existing and new medicines. NICE reviews evidence on the effectiveness of drugs; it also takes into account their costs to determine whether a particular drug offers value for money. The medical profession is expected to take these recommendations into account when prescribing treatments although the recommendations are not intended to replace the clinical judgement of medical practitioners.

## Box 1: NICE guidelines for anxiety

NICE has not yet published guidelines for social anxiety disorder. Its guidelines for the management of anxiety (published in 2004 and amended in 2007) cover panic disorder and generalized anxiety disorder in adults. It recommends three types of treatment, which are listed in order of the strength of evidence for their long-term efficacy. The first type of treatment is cognitive behaviour therapy (CBT). This should be delivered by trained and supervised people; it should mostly take the form of weekly sessions of 1–2 hours, with an optimal range of 7–14 hours, and be completed within four months. Briefer or more intensive treatment over a shorter time period might be appropriate for some patients. The second type of treatment is pharmacology, and here SSRIs are recommended. Any use of benzodiazepines should only be a short-term intervention that should not last longer than two to four weeks; they should not be prescribed for the treatment of panic disorder. Details of pharmacological treatments are the focus of this chapter. Finally, guided self-help is the third form of treatment. This draws upon self-help workbooks, based upon CBT principles; the guidelines also recommend providing patients with information about available support groups. If one type of treatment does not work for a particular patient the health care professional can try another type in discussion with the patient.

*Continued*

> The guidelines recommend that treatment should take place in primary care practice – community based health services such as family doctors (GPs), NHS walk-in centres and NHS Direct – rather than in hospital. NICE argues that this fits with many patients' preferences and results in fewer withdrawals from treatment.
>
> The guidelines emphasize 'shared decision making' between health care professional and patient, where the patient is given information about the treatment options available, what is their nature and course and information about medication where this is appropriate, including possible side effects, so that the patient can be involved in selection of treatment and throughout its course. Finally, there is emphasis on recommending treatments on the basis of the strength of scientific evidence. The implication of the recommendations is that the evidence for psychological therapy, specifically CBT, is strongest. We have explained the procedures of CBT in chapters 7 and 8.

There is increasing emphasis in medicine upon evidence-based treatment, that is to say, upon the systematic evaluation of the effectiveness of a given form of treatment. The preferred method of evaluation is the randomized control trial, where members of a sample of patients are prescribed either the drug that is under investigation or an alternative form of treatment, which could be a placebo – this is a pill or procedure that has no medical properties. Clearly, this is superior to giving treatment to only one group since you could not be sure whether it is the properties of the medicine or simply the fact that the patient is receiving any form of treatment that is effective. Indeed, studies of medication for social anxiety disorder have shown that many patients in the placebo condition do show substantial improvement in their condition. The trial is called random because participants are assigned to either a treatment or a control (placebo) condition at random. This will help control for any differences within the sample of patients, for example in the severity of their condition or the length of time that they have suffered from it. A sophisticated variation of this research design involves a double-blind procedure where the clinicians are unaware as to which condition an individual is assigned, whether he or she has been administered medication or a placebo. Neither the clinician nor the patient knows which treatment has been given.

The study aims to show that patients who have been administered the target drug show greater improvement in their condition than the control or placebo group. This is a powerful method for confirming the effectiveness of a treatment. It can be, and is applied to psychological forms of treatment, including cognitive behaviour therapy. The method does lend itself particularly well to researching pharmaceutical treatment because the double-blind procedure can more easily be set up, effects of individual differences among doctors can be controlled for, and dosage levels can be accurately measured. Nevertheless, the method has limitations. Randomized control trials are typically expensive to conduct. It can be difficult to decide what counts for a good measure of improvement. The trial may not last long enough to establish long-term effects of the treatment or to identify possible side effects of longer-term medication. Where research using this method has been published, we will report on the effectiveness of particular forms of treatment.

## What drugs are used in the treatment of social anxiety disorder?

### The SSRIs

WHAT ARE SOME NAMES OF THESE DRUGS?

There are several different Selective Serotonin Reuptake Inhibitors (and a more recent development, Serotonin and

Norepinephrine Reuptake Inhibitors – SNRI – of which venlafaxine is an example). Some that have been investigated for
the treatment of social anxiety disorder are listed below along
with some common brand names.

| Drug | Brand names |
| --- | --- |
| fluoxetine | Prozac |
| fluvoxamine | Faverine |
| | Luvox |
| paroxetine | Paxil |
| | Seroxat |
| sertraline | Lustral |
| | Zoloft |

## WHAT IS THE RATIONALE FOR THEIR USE?

These drugs work by altering the levels of a chemical, serotonin
(5-hydroxytryptamine or 5-HT), which occurs naturally in the
brain and acts as a neurotransmitter (see Box 2 for additional
details of neurotransmitters). SSRIs inhibit the reuptake of
serotonin, thereby making more of it available for neurotransmission, without affecting the reuptake of other neurotransmitters. Groups of serotoninergic neurons in the raphe nuclei
of the brainstem project onto (make contact with) a large number of target neurons in many sites of the brain. These neurons
have a coordinating and modulator role across widespread
regions of the brain, including sites known to be involved in
mood and emotion, and variations in the level of serotonin
have been shown to have many and complex effects on mood,
emotion, and behaviour. They are associated with a number of
psychological characteristics: quality of mood, feelings of self-
esteem, sexual activity, and level of arousal. Serotonin has an
overall inhibitory effect and low circulating levels result in the
individual being less able to cope with stress, less effective in
social behaviour, and more prone to impulsive aggression. Low

levels of circulating serotonin have been linked with increased irritability, mood change, increased impulsivity and risk-taking, and a tendency among depressed patients to suicidal behaviour. Low levels of serotonin are associated with depressed mood while increasing levels of serotonin are associated with more positive mood.

## Box 2: Neurotransmitters

To understand how SSRIs work it is important to know something about chemical compounds known as neurotransmitters, which play a key role in the functioning of the brain. The brain is made up of some 100,000 million cells – no one knows what is the exact figure except that it is very, very large. All these brain cells make connections with huge numbers of other cells, and the complex activity of the brain involves circuits of these connections and the transmission of information from one cell to another. Cells are separated from one another by a gap or cleft, called a synapse, and the electrical impulses which carry messages from one cell to another must cross this cleft. They do so by means of chemical transmitters. These transmitters are synthesized within brain cells and are stored in synaptic vesicles until they are released into the synapse. In order to send a message from one cell to another – from the presynaptic cell to the postsynaptic cell – an electrical impulse travels from the cell neuron along an axon (or nerve fibre) of the presynaptic cell. When the impulse reaches the end of the axon, the transmitter chemical is released and travels across the synaptic cleft. The chemical binds with receptors in the postsynaptic cell. An electrical impulse is then conducted to the neuron of this (postsynaptic) cell. This can either stimulate (have an excitatory effect on) this cell or can inhibit it. After it has fulfilled this transmission function, the neurotransmitter is either broken down by enzymes or is taken back into the nerve ending of the presynaptic neuron, a process known as

*Continued*

reuptake. If levels of the transmitter are low then messages are conducted across cells less effectively. There are many chemicals that act as neurotransmitters. One type that has been extensively investigated in psychological research is the class of monoamines. These are classified into two classes: the catecholamines – dopamine, epinephrine and norepinephrine – and the indolamines – serotonin. SSRIs work by increasing the level of serotonin that is available for transmission. They do so by preventing the reuptake of serotonin into the synapse, which allows it to remain longer in the synapse, the increased concentration facilitating transmission of subsequent messages across the synapse. This is why the drug is called a reuptake inhibitor.

Drugs that affect behaviour do so by affecting transmission across the synapse. Drugs that facilitate transmission are called agonists while drugs that inhibit transmission are called antagonists. Research studies into the process of neurotransmission or into the effects of drugs on it make use of drugs that have agonistic or antagonistic properties.

Substances that give people a 'high' act as dopamine agonists, either inhibiting the reuptake of dopamine or stimulating its synthesis.

## HOW EFFECTIVE ARE SSRIS?

Several SSRIs have been investigated for their effectiveness in the treatment of social anxiety disorder. Studies of fluoxetine, fluvoxamine, paroxetine and sertraline have shown improvements in patients relative to placebo groups. These medications are members of the same class of drugs. Sometimes one is more effective for an individual patient than other members of the class are and the doctor might switch from one drug to another within the same class to see which one is more effective. It should be noted that doctors would not switch from one class of drug to another, for example, from an SSRI to an MAOI, without arranging for an interval of time of at least fourteen days to allow the first drug that was prescribed to be 'washed out' of the patient's system. This is in case the two drugs interact with one another to produce unwanted side effects.

Because they are members of the same class of drugs the SSRIs have features in common. We consider general properties of this class in the treatment of Social Anxiety Disorder. Research studies have not shown consistent superiority of one SSRI over another, though there are a number of factors to take into account when choosing the drug, for example the period of time needed to come off the treatment.

## DOSE

Typical doses in published research studies are 20 mg per day for paroxetine, 50–200 mg a day for sertraline, fluvoxamine 50 to 300 mg per day, fluoxetine 5 to 60 mg per day. It might take between two to eight weeks for the patient to experience any improvement and it is important for the patient to continue with the medication for that period of time to allow for improvements to become evident. A patient might be recommended to take the medication for several months to reduce the chances of symptoms returning; for example NICE recommendations for depression are that the patient should continue the drug treatment for at least six months after the remission of an episode of depression.

## ARE THERE SIDE EFFECTS?

In the initial stage of taking the drug some patients report feeling agitated and anxious. This is not an indication that the drug will not be effective and the patient should not give up taking it because of these feelings. These symptoms may disappear by themselves, but the doctor can adjust the initial dosage or, if the symptoms persist, switch to a different SSRI. Some patients report side effects even after this initial period. These can include nausea, diarrhoea, constipation, loss of appetite, sleep disturbances, sweating, and sexual problems. Again, the patient should discuss these with his or her doctor.

## SUICIDAL THOUGHTS

Concerns became expressed in 2003 about the prescription of SSRIs for patients under the age of eighteen years in the light of evidence suggesting an increased risk of thoughts about suicide and self-harm among young people taking this form of medication. This issue has been subject to examination by the Medicines and Healthcare products Regulatory Agency; its detailed recommendations are presented in Box 3.

We do not know whether findings of suicidal thoughts and self-harm among patients suffering from depression also apply to patients with social anxiety disorder who are following a treatment of SSRIs. However, as we have seen in chapter 7 there

---

**Box 3: SSRIs in the treatment of young people**

In December 2003 the Medicines and Healthcare products Regulatory Agency provided a summary of the available evidence and concluded that in the case of paroxetine and sertraline (and citalopram and venlafaxine, which have not been subject to randomized control trials for social anxiety disorder) the risks outweighed the benefits of the drug in treating depression among children and adolescents. The report concluded that the benefits of fluoxetine outweighed the risks. It concluded that the risks and benefits of fluvoxamine could not be assessed. The report recommended that paroxetine, sertraline, citalopram and venlafaxine should not be prescribed as a new therapy for children and young people under the age of eighteen years. However, it did advise that psychiatrists could prescribe SSRIs for patients under eighteen in certain circumstances, for example if the patient was intolerant of fluoxetine. If SSRIs were prescribed doctors would have to monitor the patient closely for any signs of self-harm or suicidal behaviours.

is comorbidity between social anxiety disorder and depression, that is to say, about one in four patients with a social anxiety disorder also suffer from depression, and so the guidelines on close monitoring of the effects of medication for depression should be followed. NICE guidelines are that antidepressants should not be the initial form of treatment for young people with mild depression. Young people with moderate to severe depression should be offered a psychological form of therapy for at least three months. Antidepressants should only be offered alongside psychological therapy and their effects should be carefully monitored by the doctor, including frequent contact with the patient and his or her parents or carers in the first month of taking the medication. See Box 1 for a summary of NICE guidelines on anxiety.

### ARE THERE WITHDRAWAL SYMPTOMS?

The SSRIs are not addictive and there is no craving for the drug. There are no unpleasant withdrawal symptoms unless the treatment is abruptly terminated, when the patient might experience some dizziness, headaches, nausea, sleep disturbance, sweating, and feelings of anxiety. These symptoms can usually be avoided if the dosage is gradually reduced over a period of weeks, rather than suddenly stopping taking the drug.

### SUMMARY

It is evident that treatment that involves SSRIs requires a close relationship between patient and doctor. The doctor has to monitor dosage levels and adjust these to meet the needs of the individual patient. The patient needs to make the doctor aware of any side effects so that the doctor can adjust dosage or make a decision as to whether to continue with this particular drug. The patient should not interrupt taking the medication or stop taking it altogether without consultation with the doctor. This will minimize any withdrawal symptoms and also help the doctor in making decisions about future treatment of the patient's social anxiety disorder.

The doctor can also advise on possible interactions with other medicines, whether these are prescription drugs, common over the counter medications like aspirin, or herbal remedies such as St John's wort. The doctor can take into account other medical conditions of the patient such as heart conditions, diabetes, or epilepsy. The doctor can take into account possible risks during pregnancy and breastfeeding.

## The MAOIs and RIMAs

### WHAT ARE SOME NAMES OF THESE DRUGS?

Phenelzine (Nadil is a brand name for this drug) is a mono-amine oxidase inhibitor (MAOI) and moclobemide (Aurorix is a brand name) is a reversible inhibitor of monoamine oxidase (RIMA). Both have been investigated in clinical trials as treatments for social anxiety disorder. Brofaromine is a drug that combines RIMA action with serotonin reuptake inhibition.

### MAOIs

**What is the rationale for their use?**

MAOIs are one of the oldest classes of antidepressant medicines and they have been applied to the treatment of social anxiety disorder since the 1970s. They too influence the activity of neuro-transmitters. Monoamine oxidase (MAO) is an enzyme that is found in the pre-synaptic cell. It is involved in breaking down the catecholamines such as dopamine into an inactive sub-stance so that less is stored in the synaptic vesicles and less is available for release into the synapse. As the name MAOI sug-gests, the drug is designed to inhibit the activity of monoamine oxidase, and hence increase the levels of catecholamines that are stored and available to act in neurotransmission. Research shows that high levels of monoamines are associated with positive mood and low levels with negative mood; administration of drugs that decrease levels of norepinephrine and serotonin increases depression whereas those that increase the levels of monoamines reduce depression

### What is the evidence for their effectiveness?

Studies that have used randomized control designs have shown that the MAOI phenelzine is associated with greater reduction in social anxiety compared with placebo conditions. However studies reported evidence of relapse after the treatment had finished. There was also evidence of patient withdrawal from the trial because of side effects.

### Dose

Randomized control studies of phenelzine have involved dosage ranging from 30 to 90 mg per day for a period of eight to twelve weeks treatment.

### Are there side effects?

There is potential for serious side effects particularly if the drug is taken with some forms of food, and patients taking the drugs have to be extremely careful about their diet. Monoamine oxidase is present in the blood where it deactivates amines that are found in food and it functions to keeps levels of amines from becoming too high, with adverse effects of raising blood pressure. Because MAOIs inhibit the breakdown of monoamines, the levels of the monoamines can become dangerously high. Patients taking MAOIs have to avoid foods and drinks that contain the chemical tyramine as consuming them can lead to a large rise in blood pressure that can be dangerous. Tyramine is found in a wide range of everyday foods and drinks including cheese, broad beans, yeast extracts such as Bovril, Oxo and

Marmite, pickled herring, caffeine, alcohol and low alcohol drinks. Patients must also avoid some common medicines including non-prescription cough medicines and cold remedies as these too can increase blood pressure.

MAOIs can also cause drowsiness which can affect driving and the operation of machinery. Other side effects that have been reported are nausea, blurred vision, and sexual problems.

MAOIs must not be used along with SSRIs and there should be a period of 'wash out' of at least two weeks before switching from one class of drug to the other. In practice, MAOIs are not the first treatment of choice for depression and tend only to be used when SSRIs have not proved effective.

### Are there withdrawal symptoms?

The MAOIs are not addictive and there is no craving for the drug. There are no unpleasant withdrawal symptoms unless the treatment is abruptly terminated, when the patient might experience extremely unpleasant symptoms including nightmares, convulsions, headaches, nausea, insomnia, sweating, and feelings of anxiety. These can usually be avoided if the dosage is gradually reduced over a period of weeks, rather than suddenly stopping taking the drug.

#### REVERSIBLF MAOIs

In an attempt to reduce some of the risks associated with diet, a class of reversible MAOIs (RIMAs) has been developed. These inhibit one form of monoamine oxidase (form A) but not another (form B). The availability of form B enables the metabolism of tyramine and avoids the diet-related problems of the irreversible MAOIs. The RIMA moclobemide has been investigated in clinical trials as a treatment for social anxiety disorder. Brofaromine combines RIMA action with serotonin reuptake inhibition and it too has been applied to the treatment of social anxiety.

**What is the evidence for their effectiveness?**

Double-blind placebo studies that have applied moclobemide to the treatment of social anxiety disorder have obtained inconsistent results for its effectiveness, showing little superiority over the placebo. Brofaromine proved superior to placebo in two studies but not in a third.

**Are there side effects?**

Although the dietary problems of the MAOIs are reduced the patient should still avoid excessive consumption of food and drinks containing tyramine. Other side effects are similar to those reported for the MAOIs, including drowsiness, and warnings about driving and operating machinery apply. Other side effects that have been reported include anxiety, headaches, dizziness, sleep problems, digestion problems, and sexual problems.

Reversible MAOIs should not be taken alongside MAOIs or SSRIs. The doctor's advice should be taken about taking other prescription and over the counter medicines as well as about other health conditions, pregnancy, and breast-feeding.

**Are there withdrawal symptoms?**

Like the MAOIs, the reversible form of the drug is not addictive and there is no craving for it once treatment has stopped. Withdrawal symptoms can be avoided if the treatment is gradually reduced over a period of weeks.

## Beta-adrenergic receptor antagonists

### WHAT ARE SOME NAMES OF THESE DRUGS?

These are commonly known as beta blockers. Atenolol and propranolol have been used in studies of social anxiety disorder.

## WHAT IS THE RATIONALE FOR THEIR USE?

Beta-adrenergic receptor antagonists (beta blockers) were originally developed for the treatment of heart conditions. They are extensively used to reduce stimulation of the heart, for example among patients suffering from angina. They inhibit activity of epinephrine and norepinephrine, which are chemicals that are involved in reactions to danger. These reactions are often called 'fight or flight' responses and are useful for preparing the body for self-protective action when faced with threat. As we saw in chapter 1 these reactions include increased heart rate, heightened blood pressure, perspiration and so on.

Beta blockers slow the heart rate and reduce blood pressure. They also reduce the symptoms of tremor, sweating, trembling, and blushing. Because of their effectiveness in reducing these symptoms they have been widely applied in the control of anxiety.

## WHAT IS THE EVIDENCE FOR THEIR EFFECTIVENESS?

Little research has evaluated their effectiveness in the treatment of Social Anxiety Disorder. Randomized control studies that have been carried out with atenolol and propranolol have reported disappointing results. Beta blockers have been widely prescribed for people suffering from specific performance anxieties, for example sports performers, professional musicians and public speakers. In these performance circumstances the period during which anxiety is experienced can be specified and beta blockers such as propranolol can reduce the symptoms of anxiety during that period. They are less useful when the period during which anxiety will be experienced is extended or uncertain.

## WHAT ARE THEIR LIMITATIONS?

There is little evidence that these drugs are useful in the treatment of social anxiety disorder. They may not be appropriate for patients suffering from chronic heart conditions or from asthma. Side effects can include dizziness, tiredness, sleep problems, digestion problems, and skin problems such as a rash.

## Benzodiazepines

### WHAT ARE SOME NAMES OF THESE DRUGS?

Diazepam (brand name Valium), clonazepam (Klonopin), and chlordiazepoxide (Librium) are commonly prescribed sedatives in the treatment of anxiety.

### WHAT IS THE RATIONALE FOR THEIR USE?

Benzodiazepines are sedatives that have been used frequently in the treatment of anxiety disorders. They work by enhancing the activity of GABA (gamma-amino-butyric-acid), which is the major neurotransmitter found at inhibitory synapses of the central nervous system. GABA, an amino acid, has inhibitory effects on axons in a variety of brain areas, including the amygdala, which plays an important role in emotion. It influences activity in the central nucleus of the amygdala, serving to reduce anxiety. It increases sleepiness and calmness, producing relaxation of muscles. The benzodiazepines have their effects through binding with GABA to decrease anxiety; a drug that is a benzodiazepine antagonist has the opposite effect of increasing anxiety.

### WHAT IS THE EVIDENCE FOR THEIR EFFECTIVENESS?

Some research involving randomized control trials has reported promising results for clonazepam in the treatment of social anxiety disorder. However, the research reported evidence of relapse after treatment.

### WHAT ARE THEIR LIMITATIONS?

The principal limitations are their side effects and their potential for abuse and addiction. There are strong reservations about using benzodiazepines because of their side effects. They produce drowsiness, particularly in combination with alcohol. They have adverse effects on memory and concentration. For these reasons, care needs to be taken when driving or operating machinery. Prolonged use increases tolerance of the drugs and dependence on them. They have potential for addiction and abuse. Severe withdrawal symptoms can be experienced when trying to come off the medication and terminating treatment should be done gradually and in consultation with a doctor. NICE guidelines on the treatment of generalized anxiety disorder recommend that any use of benzodiazepines should only be a short-term intervention that should not last longer than two to four weeks. Benzodiazepines are not recommended for the treatment of panic disorder, as described in Box 1.

## The place of medication in the treatment of social anxiety disorder

### How is effectiveness measured?

Research has shown that patients diagnosed with social phobia or social anxiety disorder can show improvements after a period on antidepressants, particularly SSRIs. How do we know this? One approach assesses the levels of anxiety that patients report by means of questionnaires. An example of a questionnaire is the Liebowitz Social Anxiety Scale.

This questionnaire asks people how much they fear and how often they would avoid each of a set of twenty-four social situations that typically create anxiety among those with social anxiety disorder. Situations include:

- eating in public;
- speaking up at a meeting;
- talking to authority figures;
- talking to people you don't know very well.

For each situation, say, eating in public, the person reports the level of fear they would feel: none, mild, moderate, or severe. They would also answer how often they would avoid that situation: never, occasionally, often or usually. The answers to each question would be converted to numerical scores, ranging from 0 to 3. For example, when rating 'eating in public' for fear a score of 0 for that item would mean that the patient reports no fear eating in public. A score of zero when rating avoidance of the situation would mean that the person would never avoid eating in public. High scores on the questionnaire mean greater fear and more frequent avoidance. A patient's scores on the questionnaire following treatment can be compared with the scores obtained on the same questionnaire before treatment.

There are alternative ways of assessing improvement. Other measures that are used involve judgements made by the doctor rather than by the patient; for example the Clinical Global Impression Scale asks the doctor to rate how much the patient's condition has improved relative to a baseline level. The level of improvement in the condition can be described as falling on a scale as either: very much improved, much improved, minimally improved, no change, minimally worse, much worse, or very much worse. Numbers can be assigned to these judgements so that the scores obtained for patients receiving the drug treatment in a randomized control trial can be compared with the scores of those receiving the placebo in the trial.

Randomized control trials and clinical studies use measures such as these to assess the degree of improvement following a course of medication. While studies do show improvement in the short term there exists less evidence on the longer-term benefits of medication; trials are expensive and time-consuming and do not necessarily follow patients over an extended period of time. Are improvements maintained over time? Are they maintained if taking the drug is stopped? Does medication produce lasting changes in the patient's behaviour? Do patients continue to find interacting with others more satisfying?

Clear NICE guidelines about the use of SSRIs and other medications for the treatment of social anxiety disorder have not yet been published. There do exist equivalent guidelines for the treatment of generalized anxiety disorder and panic disorder (see Box 1) and of depression. NICE guidelines for the treatment of generalized anxiety disorder and panic disorder recommend treatment with SSRIs that are licensed for these disorders, although these are ranked second to cognitive behaviour therapy in terms of evidence for the long-term benefits of the intervention. Guidelines for depression state that antidepressants should not be used in the initial stages of mild depression. For severe depression a combination of cognitive behaviour therapy and medication should be considered. However, the guidelines recommend that where antidepressant medication is used in the treatment of depression this should be an SSRI.

Findings about the effectiveness of medication for the treatment of depression are controversial. There are claims that research has failed to demonstrate that SSRIs are effective in producing measurable improvements in depression that are significantly greater than improvement following the administration of a placebo. Some published meta-analyses have reviewed the findings from randomized control trials and conclude that any improvements are of little significance for clinical practice. (Box 4 provides details on meta-analysis.) Not surprisingly, pharmaceutical companies have rejected this conclusion and argue that clinical experience with antidepressants does show the benefits of SSRIs. This controversy is likely to continue. NICE guidelines that antidepressants should not be used in the initial stages of mild depression and should be combined with psychological treatment for more severe cases may provide a useful guide to the treatment of social anxiety disorder, in the absence of specific guidelines for SAD.

As we saw in chapter 7, there is evidence of the effectiveness of cognitive behaviour therapy in the treatment of social anxiety disorder. Unfortunately, as we reported in chapter 6, waiting times for this form of treatment can be long, in many cases from one to two years to see an NHS therapist. The therapy requires skilled clinicians, and they are overstretched by the

## Box 4: Meta-analysis and the effectiveness of SSRIs

Meta-analysis is a method for summarizing and evaluating a number of different studies. Although these studies can vary in many ways, for example the composition of the sample of participants, the sample size, the dosage levels, etc., meta-analysis allows the researcher to assess the overall effect of a treatment. Which studies are included in the analysis is an important point. Most analyses undertake an exhaustive search of published studies. This can produce bias since researchers might be more ready to submit studies and editors more willing to publish them when they do show a positive effect of treatment. The literature may underestimate the number of trials that produce no significant improvement in the condition. Kirsch and his colleagues obtained the findings of all randomized, double-blind, placebo-controlled clinical trials involving a number of SSRIs in the treatment of depression submitted by pharmaceutical companies to the US Food and Drug administration for licensing of the drugs. The drugs involved were fluoxetine, venlafaxine, nefazodone, paroxetine, sertraline, and citalopram. No trials were found that showed significant benefits of the last two drugs. The results of meta-analysis of fluoxetine, venlafaxine, nefazodone, and paroxetine led the researchers to conclude that the differences in improvement between the SSRI and the placebo in the trials were small and were clinically significant for only the most severely depressed patients.

demands made upon their time not just in treating social anxiety disorder but in treating a range of conditions including depression, anxiety, and obsessional-compulsive disorder. Currently there are attempts to develop computer-led therapy and this might offer greater hope of prompt treatment for the future. In the current circumstances medication might offer a valuable means of dealing with the anxious person's problems. The socially anxious person will have to bear in mind potential disadvantages of this form of treatment including possible side effects. As we have emphasized throughout this chapter the patient must be prepared to work closely with his or her doctor in the successful administration of drug treatments.

## How does medication work?

A question that we don't have an answer to is how SSRIs work. It is tempting to infer from the apparent effectiveness of this treatment that social anxiety disorder is due to a deficit of serotonin which is put right by increasing the levels circulating in the brain (see Box 5, p. 188).

Logically there is no reason why the inference should follow. A medicine may reduce the symptoms of an illness without tackling its cause. A painkiller can reduce the pain associated with an illness but this does not mean that the illness is due to any deficit in the chemical active in the painkiller. Many people try to cope with their shyness and social anxiety by taking alcohol before entering the kind of situation that triggers their anxiety. They might find that they can cope better if they do so. Of course, their social anxiety is not caused by lack of alcohol. Indeed the behavioural side effects of alcohol and the risks of dependence are high and these can produce greater problems for the anxious individual in the long run than their concerns about meeting new people or speaking up in public. Research tells us that social anxiety is comorbid with alcohol problems and one reason for this may be the anxious person's temptation

Box 5: Serotonin levels and social anxiety

> The hypothesis that social anxiety is caused by a deficiency in serotonin levels is over simple and is not supported by evidence. For example, studies that manipulate levels of serotonin find that it is related to changes in mood in depressed patients but not in people who do not suffer from depression; it is related only among patients with a personal or family history of depression. Some research has aimed to show that there is a genetic component to the link between serotonin and social anxiety. Brain scanning techniques such as functional magnetic resonance imaging (fMRI) show that individuals who carry one alternative form (allele) of the gene for the promotion of serotonin transporter have greater activity in their right amygdala, part of the brain involved in fear and anxiety. An fMRI study by Furmark and his associates found that patients with social phobia who carried the short allele of the gene showed greater right amygdala activity when believing they were waiting to give a speech in public. More of this research is likely to be carried out as brain imaging becomes more widely available, although the findings are difficult to interpret given the complexity of brain circuits and it is not clear what causes what in these studies.
>
> There is evidence that cognitive behaviour therapy has an effect on brain functioning. Specifically, psychological interventions have been found to modify activity in brain circuits. Thus, changing one's thinking and maladaptive behaviour appears to change the way in which the brain works. See a review of these studies by Veena Kumari.

to take ever increasing quantities of alcohol in an attempt to cope with his or her difficulties.

SSRIs have been shown to be effective for a range of psychological problems, not just social anxiety disorder. Is it likely that these all have the same cause, a deficiency in serotonin? Many of these problems are found together – social anxiety disorder is comorbid with depression, for example, and the drugs might work by treating the comorbid condition rather than social anxiety. Yet these conditions are distinctive, as psychologists currently understand them. Social anxiety disorder is anxiety about social interaction, anxiety about what other people think of us. I might be anxious about seeing my dentist but my fears are about what he might tell me about the condition of my teeth and gums or about the treatment that I might have to undergo. This anxiety might be excessive but even though it involves my interaction with another person it would not be thought of as social anxiety disorder. A treatment to help me with this fear might be effective but it would not help me with the many kinds of meetings that are characteristic of generalized social anxiety disorder. Darwin once pointed out that a man might be brave in battle yet fearful in the company of others, and everyday experience shows us that people can be physically brave or can tackle psychologically challenging careers like being an actor, a politician, or a judge while being extremely shy. We don't yet know why this is so.

Antidepressants and anti-anxiety drugs may be effective in the case of social anxiety disorder because they reduce the symptoms of anxiety – the pounding heart, the sweating and butterflies in the stomach. We know that fear of showing these symptoms is one of the central fears of social anxiety. We also know that experiencing these symptoms is unpleasant and has unwanted consequences for social interactions. The symptoms make it difficult to think clearly in the presence of others or to attend appropriately to signs that are given by other people; for example about taking turns in conversation or signs that indicate what they think of what you have just said. A reduction in symptoms can be beneficial in making situations less threatening. This might lead to less avoidance of the situation, to less self-consciousness or to less reliance on safety behaviours. In turn, these changes can also provide opportunities to learn something about yourself and others – you learn that other people can respond positively to you. In this sense the medication can create opportunities, but there is no guarantee that these will be taken up if you are not able to change long-standing beliefs about yourself. Changing entrenched beliefs is difficult and it has to be approached in a structured way. One of the aims of cognitive behaviour therapy is to help people do this.

SSRIs might also work by bringing about a change in mood, inducing more positive affect. One of the problems with negative affect is that it leads to a bias in processing information. As we discussed in previous chapters anxious individuals have negative beliefs about themselves and about what they think other people's opinions of them are. They have negative expectations about events – expectations that are not necessarily at the conscious level – and these expectations can bring about the outcomes that anxious people fear, influencing the behaviours they adopt, for example, safety behaviours that can be counter-productive. Medication that brings about more positive affect could influence these beliefs and expectations.

Being shy, anxious or feeling 'down' or 'blue' are all states of mind that are accompanied by bodily states that depend on the nervous system, the brain and the activity of neurotransmitters such as serotonin, dopamine, epinephrine and norepinephrine. These bodily states are unpleasant and can come to be feared in their own right. Being shy or anxious also involves thoughts and beliefs about the self and other people. These beliefs are unwelcome and intrusive and they too involve activity of the nervous system, the brain, and the neurotransmitters. Pharmaceutical treatments do produce changes in mood and anxiety but whether these changes are enduring and how they relate to the causes of depression and severe anxiety are questions for future research.

## Controversies about medication

There are controversies in government, medical research and the media about the use of SSRIs for the treatment of mental health problems including social anxiety disorder. A number of concerns have been expressed.

- One concern is the large number of prescriptions of SSRIs. In 2008 the Liberal Democrat leader Nick Clegg made a speech where he reported that thirty-one million prescriptions of antidepressant drugs had been issued in Britain in 2006. He made the point that many of these prescriptions may be issued not because they provide the most effective treatment but because of the lengthy waiting lists for alternative treatments such as cognitive behaviour therapy. The British government announced initiatives in July 2007 that are intended to speed up access to cognitive behaviour therapy, acknowledging the need to tackle the high incidence in the community of mental health problems such as anxiety disorders and depression and recognizing the benefits that CBT can bring. In February 2008, as we were writing this chapter, the Health Secretary followed up this initiative with an announcement of plans for investment in a major programme to train an additional 3,600 psychological therapists. Again this programme aims to improve access to cognitive behavioural therapies.
- A second concern is the active role of pharmaceutical companies in promoting the application of SSRIs to the treatment of social anxiety disorder. Critics question the motives behind this extension of antidepressant medication to social anxiety disorder, the appropriateness of this form of treatment for social anxiety, and the quality of the evidence demonstrating its effectiveness.
- A third concern is the quality of evidence supporting the

effectiveness of SSRIs in the treatment of depression, as we discussed above (see also Box 4).

• A fourth concern is the administration of antidepressant medication to children and young people – Clegg claimed that 631,000 prescriptions had been issued for children in 2006. As we have seen, concerns about the possible effects on suicidal thoughts have led to the issue of NICE guidelines on the restriction of their application to the treatment of children and young people.

Medication continues to be a common form of treatment for social anxiety disorder and is likely to continue to do so for some time, despite the concerns that have been expressed and the lack of knowledge about the basis of their effectiveness. The difficulties of obtaining access to psychological forms of therapy will contribute to this reliance on medication. We hope that this chapter has explained the kinds of treatment that are currently available and has drawn your attention to some of the controversies about their use. It will be valuable to have NICE guidelines on the treatment of social anxiety disorder when they are published. To conclude, the effective application of medication involves prescription-only drugs. It is essential that this treatment, including any changes in medication or termination of its use, is followed under the close guidance of a doctor or other appropriate and suitably qualified health professional.

## Key points

• A number of pharmacological treatments are available for social anxiety disorder. These medications were not originally developed for the treatment of SAD but there is evidence from randomized control trials of their effectiveness.

- Selective Serotonin Reuptake Inhibitors (SSRIs) are the most widely used medication in the treatment of generalized social anxiety disorder. They can be effective in producing quite quick changes in social anxiety symptoms.
- A number of different forms of SSRIs are available. Doctors may recommend changing from one SSRI to another in order to maximize effectiveness or to control any side effects. SSRIs are not interchangeable with other forms of medication such as MAOIs, and a period of time has to elapse before the patient switches from one class of medication to the other.
- There is concern about potential side effects of SSRIs, particularly the possibility of greater likelihood of suicidal thoughts among young people suffering from depression who are taking this medication. Guidelines have been issued to doctors about the treatment with SSRIs of young people
- The patient's doctor has a critical part to play in the management of treatment with SSRIs.
- The class of drugs known as the MAOIs has been applied to the treatment of depression and social anxiety disorder.
- MAOIs are not the first choice of treatment because of their potential for serious side effects.
- Because of these side effects MAOIs have largely been superseded by Reversible MAOIs. These are less commonly used in the treatment of social anxiety disorders than are SSRIs.
- MAOIs and Reversible MAOIs are not interchangeable with other forms of medication such as SSRIs, and a period of time has to elapse before the patient switches from one class of medication to the other.
- The patient's doctor has a critical part to play in the management of treatment with all these forms of antidepressant medication.
- Beta blockers have been widely applied to the treatment of anxiety symptoms. They are often prescribed for people

suffering from specific performance anxieties, when the period during which anxiety is experienced can be specified. They are less useful when the period during which anxiety will be experienced is extended or uncertain.

- Benzodiazepines are widely used in the treatment of anxiety symptoms. The principal limitations of their use in social anxiety disorder are their possible adverse side effects and their potential for abuse and addiction.
- Beta blockers and benzodiazepines are prescription-only drugs and should only be taken under medical supervision.
- Little is known about how antidepressant medication works in the alleviation of social anxiety disorder. They might work by altering mood or by controlling symptoms of anxiety. Further research is needed to investigate this.
- The application of antidepressant medication to social anxiety disorder is controversial. Further research is needed before these issues can be fully understood. Nevertheless there are concerns about how widespread the prescription of medication is for mental health problems, including social anxiety.

# 10

# Fear of blushing

## Blushing and social anxiety

We are devoting a separate chapter to blushing and the fear of blushing for several reasons.

First, many people see their blushing as the principal cause of their concerns. They do not regard themselves necessarily as shy or as socially anxious and believe that if they did not blush so often or so visibly they would not experience the difficulties that they do. Even when anxiety about blushing coincides with other components of shyness and social anxiety the blushing can cause the greatest concern because it is visible and because it is uncontrollable, whereas other components of anxiety can be masked or controlled in one way or another.

Second, for many people their blushing causes them serious problems in their everyday life. They feel uncomfortable all the time when they are in company because they don't know when they might suddenly redden. A blush is difficult – perhaps impossible – to prevent or to control once it has started.

Anxieties are heightened not only by the awareness that blushing is uncontrollable but also because simply thinking about blushing can induce it or intensify it. You may take steps to conceal your blushing through the use of cosmetics or by choosing clothing to minimize the skin area that is exposed. Some people take more extreme actions, avoiding all those social situations which, they anticipate, might cause them to blush. In short, the fear of blushing is a common source of anxiety about social situations. Such concerns lead many people to seek professional help and fear of blushing – erythophobia – is a presenting problem familiar to general practitioners and clinicians.

A third reason for singling out this problem is that medical research seems to hold out the promise of simply avoiding these difficulties by means of a surgical procedure which prevents the reddening of the face and neck from ever happening. While dealing with social anxiety through medication is common, as discussed in chapter 9, dealing with it through surgery is not, and the procedure deserves careful consideration. What are its advantages? Are there disadvantages? For example, does the procedure have any unwanted side effects?

On the other hand, we should emphasize that we are not allocating the topic a separate chapter because we believe it is different from shyness and social anxiety disorder in any fundamental way. We shall see in this chapter that anxieties about blushing are in fact similar to the anxieties of shyness and social anxiety disorder. We also believe that the factors that maintain all these anxieties are similar and that methods of treatment that prove successful for social anxiety disorder will also be effective for concerns about blushing.

Before discussing anxieties about blushing in more detail and how they might be overcome it will be useful to consider what a blush is in physiological terms as well as the circumstances in which we blush. Our discussion includes positive functions of the blush, though people who are anxious about their blushing are unlikely to see any positive benefits of the blush – it is something they wish to get rid of. Yet there are benefits of blushing: if there weren't any, there is no reason to think that anyone would ever blush. Why would they?

First, as we have suggested above, it is important to emphasize that fear of blushing is not something that is separate from shyness or social anxiety disorder. What is the evidence for this? Let's first consider shyness. Very many people say that they blush whenever they feel shy and many shy people report blushing to be a major symptom of their shyness. About half of the people who completed the Stanford Shyness Survey described in chapters 2 and 3 said that blushing was a symptom of their shyness. Indeed, blushing was the most commonly reported physical symptom.

There is considerable similarity between social anxiety disorder and chronic blushing problems although, as we suggested at the beginning of this chapter, some of those with blushing problems identify their facial reddening as the principal cause of their problem. They do not believe that it is a sign or symptom of an underlying shyness or anxiety. What is the connection between fear of blushing and social anxiety disorder? Can you have one without the other? We can approach these questions in two ways. One approach asks whether people

### Box 1: Blushing and shyness

Ishiyama found that the majority of a sample of adolescents reported blushing whenever they felt shy, whether or not they thought of themselves as shy: the frequency of reports was not very different among those who described themselves as shy (seventy-one per cent of shy participants reported blushing when shy) from the frequency among those who did not think of themselves as shy people (sixty-one per cent of these said they blushed when they felt shy). These data indicate that blushing often accompanies shyness.

who are anxious about their blushing meet diagnostic criteria for social anxiety disorder. In one study participants were approached via the Internet websites of newsgroups whose members expressed interest in surgical treatment to prevent blushing. They completed a questionnaire based on standard criteria for social anxiety disorder. It was found that more than half (sixty per cent) of participants who had blushing concerns met the criteria for social anxiety disorder. About half of those who reported problems with both blushing and sweating met the criteria for social anxiety disorder.

We can approach the question from the opposite direction and ask whether patients with social anxiety disorder report problems with blushing. Research has shown that concerns about blushing are reported much more frequently by patients with social anxiety disorder than by those diagnosed with other anxiety conditions, for example, agoraphobia. On the other hand, there is no difference between patients diagnosed with social anxiety disorder and patients with other anxiety disorders in the frequency of other common anxiety symptoms such as palpitations, dry mouth, sweating, trembling, and feeling hot or cold. For many people who meet diagnostic criteria for social anxiety disorder, blushing is much more of a problem than any other physiological symptoms. There is also evidence that individuals with generalized social anxiety disorder report more problems with blushing than do those with the non-generalized type.

In summary, significant numbers of people who are anxious about their blushing meet diagnostic criteria for social anxiety disorder and a substantial proportion of individuals who have been diagnosed with social anxiety disorder report blushing as a serious concern. Nevertheless, the research does show that blushing can be a problem in its own right for many people, in that they report blushing concerns without reporting other anxieties. What is it about blushing that disturbs them? For example, do they blush more often or more intensely than other people do? Before we try to answer this question let us think about what a blush is.

## What is a blush?

### The physiology of the blush

What physiological mechanisms are involved in blushing? Variation in blood flow through subcutaneous capillaries in the face and other areas where reddening occurs – the 'blush region' – is related to temperature control and is regulated by centres in the hypothalamus responsible for body temperature. When temperature rises, for example, when we take part in physical exercise, the capillaries are opened (a process called vasodilation) and there is an increased flow of blood closer to the surface of the skin. This allows cooling of the blood and brings about a reduction in body temperature.

We are an essentially hairless species and we rely on the circulation of blood close to the skin, particularly at the face, hands, and feet, in order to cope with environmental changes in temperature and to maintain the temperature of the brain and the other principal internal organs at a constant level. Because of its key role in temperature regulation the system of skin blood vessels has a distinctive, specialized structure which enables a substantial volume of blood to flow close to the skin so that heat can be lost. For details of this, see Box 2.

We can see that the so-called blush region has a structure that lends itself to reddening. There are several causes of facial reddening in addition to the blush. For example, if we press something against the skin of the face, this will produce reddening due to an increase in blood flow in that area: extra blood is sent to that region to compensate for loss of nourishment during the compression. Consumption of alcohol can also produce reddening of the face.

Box 2: Physiology of the blush

> Blood flows along the arteries and resistance vessels (smaller arteries and arterioles) in the subcutaneous layer into the capillaries in the epidermis. These form loops under the dermis before flowing via the venules into an extensive network of veins, the venous plexus. This network carries a large proportion of the volume of blood that flows close to the skin. The subcutaneous arteries have direct links to the venous plexus via vessels known as arteriovenous anastomoses, so that blood can be 'shunted' directly from arterioles to venules without passing through the capillary beds, thereby facilitating blood flow by reducing resistance.
>
> The blush region has a distinctive anatomical structure that lends itself to reddening. Facial skin has large numbers of capillary loops in the dermis, the venous plexus – an extensive network of veins in the subcutaneous layer – holds a large amount of blood and the blood vessels are close to the surface of the cheek. The increased blood flow is apparent in the reddening of the skin that we notice on a hot day or that typically accompanies physical exercise. Redness of the skin is caused by engorgement of the capillaries in the dermis with blood, and the colour is due to haemoglobin, the pigment that carries oxygen in the blood.

While the role of facial reddening in temperature control and nourishment is reasonably well understood, little is known about *why* a blush occurs, that is, why facial reddening occurs in certain circumstances that seem to have little to do with temperature control and more to do with our emotions.

Physiologically, there is emerging evidence that the blush is produced by heightened sympathetic activity of the autonomic nervous system. Heightened sympathetic activity is central to the system regulating emotion. More specifically, there is evidence that blushing is mediated by specific receptors in the facial area, know as beta-adrenergic receptors. There is a high density of these receptors in the facial veins. Sympathetic arousal of these receptors produces vasodilation. Lesions to the sympathetic pathway to the face or surgical disruption of the sympathetic chain (which we discuss in a later section on surgical interventions for blushing anxiety) prevent reddening from occurring.

As we have seen in earlier chapters heightened sympathetic nervous system activity has a major role in emotion: its involvement explains many emotional reactions involved in fear, including increased heart rate, sweating, and trembling. As we have seen, these symptoms are reported by shy people and those diagnosed with social anxiety disorder. Reddening of the face can accompany other intense emotions such as anger, although we call this flushing rather than blushing, and a blush feels rather different from the angry flush. What is it that specifically produces what we experience as a blush? Perhaps understanding the circumstances in which a blush is likely to occur can give us a clue as to its nature.

## The circumstances of blushing

The most common explanation for blushing is that it is an expression of embarrassment. Certainly we often blush when we are embarrassed, and the situations where people describe themselves blushing are similar to those where they describe themselves being embarrassed. Both types of situations involve feeling self-conscious. Both involve believing that you are the object of other people's attention; as Charles Darwin wrote in a famous essay on the blush, 'it is the thinking of what others think of us which excites a blush'.

Circumstances that make us blush include:

- Breaking a social 'rule' or convention; for example being dressed inappropriately for an occasion, saying the wrong thing at the wrong time, or forgetting someone's name when you come to introduce them.

- Behaving ineptly, such as tripping up or spilling a drink in front of other people:

  > I made a hash of parking the car when two male council workers were sat in their lorry waiting for something.

  A seven-year-old boy gave the following example of someone blushing:

  > Somebody tripped over when they were in a football match. They were embarrassed because I think they would be upset because they were doing so well and then they trip over.

- Losing control over bodily functions, for example audibly passing wind in the presence of others, or over your appearance, as when you realize your zip is undone.
- Breaching privacy, for example when discussing sexual matters, having to describe symptoms of an intimate nature to a doctor, or having information about a personal matter being revealed:

  > Something personal was told to a teacher by a friend. I was embarrassed that he knew about my personal life.

- Behaving out of character or role, for example being over-heard making a derogatory remark about someone who thinks that you are their friend.
- Being praised, complimented or thanked; this is more likely to induce a blush when there is an audience, but this is not necessary:

  > My boss told me he valued my work. I was embarrassed, didn't know how to respond.

- Feeling conspicuous; this is a cause of blushing such that you may colour simply because you are the centre of attention or fear being so. For example being asked a question in class, having your name called out in public, or entering a room where everyone present has already taken their seats.

> A comedian entertaining a large audience in the theatre asked people from particular cities to raise their hand and when they did so he would make a funny remark. When he mentioned my city I didn't dare put up my hand but I blushed anyway. Which was silly because no one would know where I was from.

- Being told you are blushing. This can often induce blushing by itself, in the absence of any other circumstances; once you are aware of your blushing this can sustain it, as the following example shows:

> Someone said that I fancied a particular boy. I blushed because I didn't know anybody else had realised this. Someone said, 'you're going red'. Which obviously made it worse.

All of these circumstances can readily be understood as giving rise to embarrassment as we described it in chapter 3, to its sense of fluster and uncertainty how to behave, the self-consciousness and the feeling of being out of place that it entails.

Yet perhaps it is not accurate to regard embarrassment and blushing as the same. You can be embarrassed without necessarily blushing. Psychologists have carried out very detailed micro-analysis of video-recordings of people who are embarrassed. They have identified a typical display of the emotion. This involves a rapid sequence of events: glancing at and away from the other person present; an involuntary smile; an attempt to control the smile. This research does not regard the blush as an integral part of this display.

It might be more productive to be more specific about the circumstances that produce a blush, and two ideas have been proposed: that blushing is a response to unwanted attention from others; that the blush occurs when something private about the self has been exposed, or is at risk of being exposed. An eight-year-old boy shows awareness of this:

*Do you know what blushing is?*
Yes

*What is it?*
You go red.

*Can you think of an example when someone might blush?*
If they have been naughty and they are trying not to get anyone to see but then someone saw and they might blush.

*Can you think of any other times?*
If they have to do something all by themselves with lots of people and they get it wrong.

Charles Darwin has written on the importance of attention in blushing:

> whenever we know, or suppose, that others are depreciating our personal appearance, our attention is strongly drawn toward ourselves, more specifically to our faces ... whenever we know, or imagine, that any one is blaming, though in silence, our actions, thoughts, or character; and, again, when we are highly praised.

In recent times the psychologist Mark Leary has developed this notion, arguing that we blush when we receive unwanted attention that we cannot escape from. We can extend this definition in two ways. First, to circumstances where the person anticipates that they will receive unwanted attention – the blush can precede the attention and indeed can actually bring it about. For example, I might blush when a particular topic is mentioned in a group conversation and in doing so bring everyone's attention to me. Second, the unwanted attention can take the form that some private information about the self may be revealed to others. Perhaps others find out something we don't want them to know. Or we believe, rightly or wrongly, that someone else knows already or might be just about to learn something about us that we would rather they did not know.

Many of our examples reflect this notion of exposure of some aspect of the self to public view: the student who doesn't want personal information known to her teacher; the child who has been naughty and whose naughtiness is exposed. We can also blush when we think that people might think something about us even though it is not true. A child might blush because she thinks the teacher might believe she had been the naughty one, even though she hadn't. Indeed, the teacher might seize upon the blush as evidence that the child had been the naughty one.

This allows us to think about the connections between shyness or social anxiety and the blush. Much of the behaviour associated with shyness is to do with hiding avoiding making eye contact with someone, keeping in the background, concealing your true opinions on a matter under discussion. When you are shy you are quiet and hesitant to join in because you fear that you will reveal something about yourself that would lead others present to have a less favourable opinion of you. What you fear that you will reveal can be your lack of competence in, say, a work issue; or it may be what you think of as your lack of social competence that you wish to keep from others. This perspective on shyness has emerged in anthropological research that has aimed to identify the language of emotions in different societies across the world.

Shyness is the emotion when:

I don't know what things are good to do/say here
I don't want to do/say something bad
I don't want people to think something bad about me

You may colour when you are asked a question because you fear that your answer will reveal your inadequacies or even that simply having the attention drawn to you will reveal them. You fear that people will 'think something bad about you'. For a similar reason, being praised or thanked may raise concerns in you about your feeling of unworthiness – if they knew the real you or how you owed your success to luck rather than to your abilities – they might not think so highly of you. Shyness is not simply doubting yourself but fearing that your supposed inadequacies will be revealed to others.

## The blush as a signal

This analysis of the blush begins to suggest how it is an unpleasant experience. It is to do with being exposed in the eyes of others. It can be a shaming experience and shame and humiliation are among our worst feelings. But our analysis raises one of the paradoxes of the blush – its visibility. Our red face makes us conspicuous at the very moment when we would prefer to be hidden; we become more visible just at the moment when we wish the ground would open up and swallow us. Why should our reaction to being exposed or our expression when we are embarrassed be accompanied by a highly visible facial display?

One answer to this is to consider the blush as a form of communication. It signals something to others. What does it signal, and why? One answer is that the blush acts as an apology or a gesture of appeasement. What you are communicating when you blush is that you acknowledge that whatever has happened to cause you to blush is wrong in some way *and* that you are sorry for it. A blush serves a positive function for the person who is embarrassed and for everyone involved in the predicament that has given rise to the blush. This has advantages for everyone concerned. If the blush is effective in communicating this apology, it will be less likely that the others will react aggressively or will reject the person who is held responsible.

This may become clearer with an example, one that has been studied in psychological research. Say, you walk right up to the sales counter in a busy shop, in doing so you go to the front of a queue of people who are waiting for their turn to make their purchases. It is likely that they will be angry with you, thinking you are selfish or rude, and some might make comments or remonstrate with you. If you realize that you have unintentionally jumped the queue you can deflect this criticism by making an apology: a blush is an effective means of doing this since it shows that you acknowledge that you have done wrong. The uncontrollable nature of the blush makes it a particularly effective signal since it represents an apology that cannot be faked and hence is more likely to be regarded as sincere. These types of incidents have been studied and it has been found that people are judged more positively and the situation is judged to be less serious if the person is described as either verbally apologizing or blushing: a blush without an apology is just as effective as a verbal apology.

This is an important consequence of the blush that is often overlooked when we concentrate on it as an unpleasant expression of emotion or when we emphasize the fear of blushing that many individuals experience. The blush has a part to play in social life. I might prefer to redden less often or less visibly than I do. But if no one ever blushed imagine how difficult it would be to get on with other people?

There is an alternative answer to the question why we blush – we do so because it is valuable for getting on with one another.

## Anxieties about blushing

We all blush at one time or another. We have a good idea of the circumstances that lead to a blush. Yet some people are much more bothered about their blushing than others are. They can be upset to the extent that they seek treatment to reduce or stop their blushing altogether. What is the reason for these anxieties? Is it that some people blush more often than others do? Or blush more intensely? It is possible that some people do blush more conspicuously and this heightens their self-consciousness. For example, some people's skin complexion might make facial reddening more visible and this might lead them to believe that they blush more conspicuously than others do. This can make them more self-conscious and this in turn may make blushing more likely and more unpleasant. There is evidence for this:

- Research shows that individuals who believe they blush more often than others do are more likely than those who think they blush less often to report that they have a fair or very fair complexion; this contrasts with those who claim they blush less often than others do, who are more likely to report that they have natural tan or dark skin. Interestingly, there is no association between complexion and self-reported reddening of the skin during non-blushing episodes such as physical exercise, alcohol consumption, drinking warm liquids or being in a hot environment.
- We can also consider differences between ethnic groups in the predominant lightness and darkness of skin complexion – the blush would be less visible in a darker complexion. Blushing is reported more frequently to be a symptom of embarrassment in Britain than it is in Mediterranean countries. People with darker complexion tend to refer more to skin temperature than to facial reddening when commenting on their blushing.

Yet there is more to concern about blushing than complexion. Surveys reveal individual differences in people's reports about their frequency of blushing. Surveys also show individual differences in fear of showing symptoms such as blushing, sweating and trembling. Some people report greater levels of fear of these symptoms. They also describe the strategies that they adopt to cope with their fears, for example avoidance strategies or attempts to mask their symptoms. There is no doubt that these anxieties are widespread and intensely felt. But why do so many people have these anxieties? Do they have a physiological basis? Do they blush more often or more intensely than others do? We don't have a lot of evidence but the evidence we do have suggests that there is not a physiological basis for these differences.

An important finding emerges from research that examines the actual blushing of people who say they are more likely to blush than others or who report greater fear of blushing. There is little evidence that they do blush more than others, when this is measured physiologically or when others observe their behaviour. See Box 3 for this research.

We must be careful not to generalize from what is still a very small number of studies. Nevertheless, the evidence points to the source of the fear of blushing in beliefs about blushing rather than in physiological differences. This is important to bear in mind when thinking about effective treatments. Should treatment focus on changing beliefs or on the physiology? Yet the

## Box 3: Physiological measures and beliefs about blushing

Mulkens and colleagues found little relation between physiological measures of the intensity of blushing and scores obtained on blushing questionnaires or self-reports of the extent of blushing. There is no relation between measures of tendencies to blush or fear of blushing and an increase in cheek coloration, facial temperature or skin conductance when these physiological measures are taken while participants are engaged in an embarrassing task. There is no relation between self-report questionnaire measures of propensity to blush and fear of blushing and ratings of people's blushing made by observers of their behaviour. People with high scores on the questionnaire measures report that they blush more even though neither the physiological data nor the reports of observers show that they do actually blush more. Differences between blushers and non-blushers are not found on physiological measures: the differences are in beliefs about blushing. The only physiological difference that has been found is when high scorers on blushing questionnaires are provided with feedback that they are blushing: this feedback is associated with a measurable increase in blood flow.

fact remains that people *are* anxious about their blushing so we cannot totally separate psychology from physiology. One model that aims to bring these together proposes that interpersonal situations evoke anxiety that produces self-focused attention. This self-focus makes anxious individuals more sensitive to changes in their bodily states, including cues that they are blushing, for example, a felt change in skin temperature. This, in turn, increases their tendency to focus on themselves and intensifies their fear of blushing. This leads them to overestimate the extent of their blushing. We have seen that evidence does show that individuals who obtain high scores on measures of fear of blushing and blushing propensity do overestimate their blushing and embarrassment relative to individuals with low scores. Despite this, their estimations do not seem to relate reliably to physiological measures of facial temperature or colour changes that presumably represent actual facial flushing.

Even if the fear of blushing is related to exaggeration of the extent of actual blushing, what is it that is feared? What is wrong with being seen to blush? Blushing is thought to be likely to attract the attention of others and to reveal to them that the person is not comfortable, poised or in control of the situation. The blusher may believe that this is a sign of 'silliness', nervousness, weakness or immaturity, appearing 'weird'. A man may believe that his blushing shows he is less masculine, where masculine means to be strong and in control. You might think that others will not take you seriously if you are blushing, or it may undermine the impression you are tying to make. It makes your anxieties visible: you can often hide these from people but it is difficult to do when your face, ears and neck go red. As is the case for shyness and social anxiety, what others think is very important. The fear that you will blush becomes salient and this can become a self-fulfilling prophecy. It may not be helped if other people draw attention to your blush, as a comment or as a tease. This too heightens self-consciousness.

Case 1

> Nicholas was in his thirties and divorced. He was lonely and desperate to start another relationship. He went to bars and social events to meet women but he felt that he was rejected on every occasion because he always blushed whenever he tried to speak to a woman. The blush would come on at once and he couldn't stop it. He was convinced that blushing was not compatible with being a man and that women would regard him as weak and not masculine. This affected his confidence about approaching women.

When you are anxious about blushing, the blush can be an intensely unpleasant experience. It is accompanied by the negative thoughts and feelings that are characteristic of social anxiety more generally. You are self-conscious, you cannot think clearly, you don't know what to say or you gabble, you wish to escape the situation. Internet websites devoted to social anxiety and fear of blushing present vivid stories describing the miseries that blushing causes many people. By suggesting that fear of blushing is a matter of belief more than physiology we do not intend to minimize the suffering that is experienced. Rather, it is to suggest one possible means of overcoming these intense fears.

## The treatment of fear of blushing

### The cognitive approach

Those who are anxious about their blushing often adopt strategies that are intended to minimize the visibility of their blush. You can apply cosmetics, for example wearing a green cream under your foundation so that the green will help neutralize the redness. Or you can wear high necked clothing or adopt hairstyles that cover part of the face. You can wear clothing that is cool, avoid warm parts of the room, or keep out of broad daylight or remain in darker corners, all to make the face less visible. The reader might recognize these strategies as examples of safety behaviours. As we discussed in chapter 7 the problem with safety behaviours is that they actually work to maintain high levels of anxiety. They can even make the feared outcome more likely to occur. It makes people anticipate blushing and this tends to bring the blush on. It heightens self-awareness of the blush and thereby intensifies it. Or acting in an odd way can attract the unwanted attention of others. As we have seen, helping patients with social anxiety to identify and challenge safety behaviours plays a key role in the cognitive approach to the treatment of social anxiety disorder.

The cognitive approach to treating fear of blushing based on cognitive behaviour therapy is similar to the approach discussed in chapters 7 and 8. The cognitive approach focuses on challenging negative beliefs about blushing and its consequences. It encourages the client to analyse such self-statements as 'blushing means that you hide something' or 'blushing makes you look stupid'. It involves systematic, gradual exposure to the kinds of situations that elicit blushing. Practice takes place during therapy sessions and in 'homework' exercises in actual social situations.

Another cognitive approach aims to reduce the self-focused attention that is associated with blushing. Patients are encouraged to focus attention on a task rather than upon themselves. The treatment aims to increase patients' understanding of the role of attention in fear of blushing. They practise focusing outwards in social situations. Exposure to these situations is managed in a systematic way. It can begin with practice in less threatening situations, for example, concentrating on the content of a news broadcast. The patient then moves on to practise external focus of attention in a typical blush-eliciting situation. Again, these situations are arranged in order from those that the patient identifies as least likely to elicit a blush to those that are more likely to do so. The exercises involve role-play during sessions and also homework practice in actual social situations. The patient attempts to tackle situations that elicit blushing without relying on avoidance strategies or on safety behaviours.

## Medication

The medications that have been applied to social anxiety disorders – the SSRIs, MAOIs, and beta blockers discussed in chapter 9 – have also been prescribed in the treatment of fear of blushing. These are not directed at blushing per se but at the anxieties that are associated with it. Reducing fear of blushing can reduce the incidence of blushing since, as we have seen, self-focused attention and awareness of blushing can bring about the blush. The advantages and limitations of this approach to treatment are discussed in chapter 7. We emphasize again that pharmacological treatments are prescribed by doctors and their management involves the close involvement of the patient's doctor.

## Surgery

There are reports in the medical literature of large-scale studies that have treated problems of blushing by a surgical procedure known as endoscopic thoracic sympathectomy. This uses endoscopic techniques to divide the sympathetic chain where it overlies the second and third rib in the upper thoracic region. Researchers have reported high rates of success in a series of articles in surgery and dermatology journals. Success is defined in terms of reduction of blushing and also in terms of reported quality of life. The technique was originally applied to problems of excessive perspiration (hyperhidrosis) but it also resulted in patients reporting reductions in facial blushing. A brief account of the research studies is presented in Box 4.

Box 4: Research into endoscopic thoracic sympathectomy

> Studies conducted by doctors Rex, Drott, Claes and their colleagues at Borås Hospital in Sweden reported the findings from 244 patients with blushing problems who had been operated on over a seven-year period. All the patients had reported blushing as 'disabling' and were screened for other causes of facial redness, for example dermatological conditions such as rosacea. Patients reported having taken medication and alcohol in attempting to deal with their blushing. Their average age was thirty-four years with a range of ages from fifteen to sixty-seven years. Questionnaires were sent to the patients after surgery: the average time of follow-up was eight months after surgery, with a range from two months to twenty-nine months. The questionnaires asked patients to report the degree of their blushing and sweating. Ninety-six per cent of these patients reported a reduced rate in blushing following surgery; eighty-five per cent expressed total satisfaction with the operation, thirteen per cent were dissatisfied to some extent, and two per cent regretted having had the operation. Over eighty per cent of respondents reported improvement in the difficulties that their blushing had previously caused them: fear of being the centre of attention, difficulties in keeping a clear mind, and avoiding social situations such as meetings at work, parties, and meeting an acquaintance on the street. The operation produced few complications or serious side effects and there were substantial and statistically significant reductions in reported fear of blushing.

The success rates reported in these studies are high. This form of treatment is now available in the NHS in the United Kingdom although there are long waiting lists. Clearly anyone considering surgical intervention for treatment should begin by consulting their general practitioner. There are several points to bear in mind:

1. The change is permanent and irreversible.
2. There are risks with any surgery performed under anaesthetic.

3. It is possible that the patient satisfaction reported a matter of months after surgery might not be maintained in the longer term, particularly if patients experience enduring side effects from the procedure or if it does not lead to greater self-confidence and less shyness and anxiety in social situations.
4. The treatment targets blushing rather than the fear of blushing.
5. The abolition of blushing ignores the positive benefits of a blush.

The first two points are matters of discussion with the general practitioner who can explain the procedure and the risks entailed. The doctor's advice would draw upon his or her knowledge of the patient's medical history, the patient's general health, any other anxieties or problems that are experienced and any medication that is being taken.

Potential side effects of the operation are a matter of concern. While the research reports that the incidence of side effects is low and patient satisfaction is high overall, the effects can be extremely distressing when they do occur. In the research studies a minority of patients report regretting having had the operation. The side effects can be unpleasant and potentially as embarrassing for the patient as the original blushing. Although the operation reduces sweating in the face, armpit, and palms of the hands, it does lead to significant compensatory increases in sweating elsewhere in the body, including the trunk and groin. It can also lead to 'gustatory' sweating associated with tastes and smells. Another possible side effect is Horner's syndrome, drooping of the eyelid, constriction of the pupil and dryness of the affected side of the face. Another possible effect is Raynaud's phenomenon. This is a condition of narrowing of the arteries carrying blood to the skin, which results in reduced circulation to the hands, experienced as pins and needles and numbness and redness of the skin.

There are several Internet forums and support groups which show that a substantial number of former patients have experienced distress and that there have been attempts to reverse the procedure to mitigate the adverse side effects. The Internet website of the Center for Hyperhidrosis does not recommend surgery for patients whose primary problem is blushing and recommends instead pharmacological treatment. It claims that the frequency of compensatory sweating is greater among patients who have undergone surgery because of facial blushing or sweating than it is among patients who are operated on for sweating hands, and argues that this is because the sympathectomy is carried out at the T2 level (the T2 ganglion is located between the second and third ribs). While other Internet sites acknowledge the benefits of the procedure in reducing shyness and anxiety, some former patients claim that they were not made fully aware that the side effects would be so severe and distressing. Several correspondents report that these side effects have impaired their life, reducing their capacity for physical exercise and leading on occasion to loss of employment. Effects mentioned include compensatory sweating, increased and irregular heart rate, shortness of breath, fatigue and depression (see the Patients Against Sympathectomy Surgery website).

Satisfaction with the procedure may be reduced over time if the operation does not lead to greater self-confidence and less shyness and anxiety in social situations. As we have noted, individuals with social anxiety often attribute the cause of their difficulties to the blush. This is a physiological reaction that is beyond their control and is in a sense 'external' to them, a matter of 'bad luck'. If social anxieties and lack of confidence persist even after blushing has been eradicated it might be particularly distressing to discover that one's social difficulties cannot be explained in this way.

Our fourth point is that treatment targets the physiology of blushing rather than the fear of blushing. The assumption underlying the approach is that blushing is the cause of the problem, that it is an inherently unpleasant experience and that patients blush more frequently or intensely than they find acceptable. However, if the problem is fear of blushing rather than blushing per se, then *this* is the problem that should be addressed, and efforts should be directed to improving psychological forms of interventions designed to reduce anxiety. As we have noted, individuals who are anxious about blushing may not in fact blush any more than others but may exaggerate the frequency and the negative consequences of their reaction.

Endoscopic thoracic sympathectomy is controversial. There are several Internet sites that provide information about the procedure and accounts given by people who have undergone the treatment including patients who are dissatisfied with its outcome. A list of these sites is included in the appendix at the end of the book.

### Where do I find treatment?

The advice we offer is similar to that provided in chapter 6. Making an appointment with your doctor is a good starting point as your GP can prescribe medication and can give access to specialist help, for example from the primary care mental health service. Cognitive behaviour therapy, counselling and forms of psychotherapy are available for anxiety about blushing. The organizations and websites we mentioned in chapter 6 also carry information about blushing. For example, a section of the SA-UK website provides helpful information on blushing that includes personal stories about the distress caused by blushing and information about the treatments that are available.

## Key points

- Many people regard their blushing as a problem in its own right, often causing deep distress. Evidence shows that anxiety about blushing tends to be associated with social anxiety disorder. Treatments that are effective for SAD can also be applied effectively to fear of blushing.

- The blush is a very common phenomenon. Facial reddening is produced by physiological changes involved in the regulation of body temperature. It also accompanies emotional states such as anger, shyness and embarrassment. It is not entirely understood why this is the case.

- One puzzle of blushing is that it often occurs in circumstances where we don't want to be noticed by others yet the change in appearance increases our visibility.

- This can be understood in terms of the positive contribution that the blush makes to the smooth running of social life. It acts as an apology and affirms the blusher's adherence to the values of the group. This is a valuable function though it is not one that is always appreciated by individuals anxious about their blushing.

- Anxiety about blushing is related to concerns about what other people think about us and therefore to social anxiety. Like social anxiety, it can lead to impairment of social functioning and reduction in the quality of life.

- Treatments that are effective for social anxiety disorder are also effective for anxiety about blushing.

- Cognitive behaviour therapy addresses the beliefs that people have about the negative consequences of their blushing. It also analyses the role that safety behaviours play in coping with blushing and encourages individuals to replace these safety behaviours with more positive strategies.

- A form of intervention distinctive to the treatment of blushing anxiety is surgery to prevent reddening from taking place. While there is research evidence for its effectiveness there are concerns about potential adverse side effects. There are also concerns about the appropriateness for irreversible surgical intervention for anxieties that may be

psychological in origin and maintained by beliefs and behaviours that can be changed.
- Treatments for anxiety about blushing are available and can be accessed by the approaches outlined in earlier chapters. The GP should be the starting point; there are several organizations that have websites, provide information on blushing, run self-help groups and provide information about therapists.

# 11

# Rounding things up

## The nature of shyness

Our starting point was that many of us feel extremely shy or anxious in social situations. We wanted this book to help you to learn more about these feelings by presenting you with information from a psychological perspective. We have focused on two concepts – shyness and social anxiety disorder – acknowledging that they overlap to a large extent.

Shyness is an everyday concept, captured by a short word that has several meanings and connotations. The word refers to a style or way of behaving in the presence of other people. It usually – but not always – refers to being quiet and restrained. There is nothing inherently negative about shyness in this sense. Shyness can be a positive description of how someone behaves: quietness can be an attractive quality, associated with calmness or willingness to listen to others. How it is regarded can depend on the situation you are in; sometimes it is more appropriate to be quiet and to be sensitive to the circumstances.

An example is meeting someone who has just suffered bereavement or who has recently learned that they are ill. At other times we think that more outgoing, less inhibited behaviours may be more appropriate, for example at a celebration, where restrained behaviour might seem more awkward and out of place. We saw in chapter 3 that different societies value shyness differently, for example in Finland it is more likely to be seen as a positive quality than it is in, say, America.

Shyness can also be a description of someone's personality. When we think about what someone is like and try to 'sum them up' we refer to their shyness when we want to indicate their tendency to be quiet, non-assertive, to keep in the back ground, to follow rather than to lead. We think that these behaviours are characteristic of the person and are not isolated responses. Again, this trait can be thought of as either a positive or a negative quality. How it is regarded seems to be influenced by cultural values, as we saw in the case of modern China where shyness has become less positively valued within a short period of time. There is evidence that the incidence of shyness is increasing within our own society, in that more and more people are prepared to label themselves as shy. It often surprises shy people how many other people also consider themselves to be shy. The evidence also suggests that many people are unhappy about their shyness and wish that they could change this part of their personality.

Shyness is not alone in seeming to have increased in incidence. Depression, autism, asthma and eating disorders are other examples of conditions that have increased greatly in our society since the 1980s. There are probably many reasons for this. Some commentators draw attention to the stresses of modern life, which make us more anxious and prone to depression. Increasing awareness of these conditions is also likely to be a factor. We don't only mean awareness in the medical profession but also across the general population. The names of these conditions offer labels which help us to make sense of our anxieties.

Other commentators express concern about our readiness to interpret these reactions to stressful circumstances as problems which are the responsibility of the individual or to regard them as medical conditions. One argument is that we are too ready to consider problems of living in modern society as medical conditions rather than address the social conditions that give rise to the problems. For example, the rise in anorexia and bulimia creates severe problems for many young people – problems that give rise to genuine distress in them and those who love them. These disorders are not known in societies that give less emphasis to appearance or that place less value on a slim physique or pay less attention to the fashion models and actors who act as role models. Cultural values do not create these conditions but they do provide an environment in which they can develop. A similar argument has been made for shyness, arguing that its social context is the value that is placed on individualism and social success brought about by being a 'personality'.

Another strand in this argument is that the pharmaceutical industry is dependent on its growth for extension of its products into new markets by their application to new disorders, for example the application of antidepressant drugs to the treatment of social anxiety disorder: this extension increases the market for producers of medication without them necessarily incurring the enormous financial costs of developing and testing new products. One version of this argument is that the condition of social anxiety disorder is itself a creation of the pharmaceutical industry, that it has influenced the medical profession to regard social anxiety as a medical condition amenable to medication. The expansion of the market for psychological medication is of course of commercial value to the manufacturers of drugs. However, this argument – whatever its rights and wrongs – does not deny the distress that social anxiety causes individuals, and the need to find ways to help people overcome these anxieties.

Our book has devoted space to consideration of the meaning of shyness, its relation to embarrassment, blushing, and modesty, and the importance of considering the positive side of these everyday experiences. We do this because we propose that there is nothing inherently wrong with being shy or socially anxious or prone to blushing. Knowing that you are shy does not mean that you should accept that you have a psychological problem or that you need treatment. Nor does being labelled as shy by other people. Often the way that shyness is described in the media gives the opposite impression, with its references to 'cures'. We have emphasized that shyness is a common and understandable reaction to particular circumstances that we all experience at one time or another. For some people, it is only experienced occasionally; for others, it seems more ingrained in their personality. It is ingrained in the same way as being impulsive or cautious is, whether you jump in or hold back, whether you tend to be nervous or confident.

## The treatment of social anxiety

When does shyness or social anxiety become a problem? There exist diagnostic criteria and self-report checklists for social anxiety disorder that can give indications and we have described these in chapters 3 and 6. However, we suggest that you ask yourself some questions that might help you decide whether you would benefit from the investment of time and effort that effective treatment demands. Does anxiety cause you significant life impairment, produce severe distress, or lower your sense of happiness and satisfaction with life?

Treatment can be of benefit if social anxiety causes impairment in your social relationships, school or work performance, leisure activities, your health or your ability to deal with the routine activities of daily living. Even if social anxiety does not impair your performance or your ability to function effectively, experiencing extreme discomfort during social events can indicate that treatment would be useful. We have seen that some people are intensely anxious in social situations even if they cope well with those situations or do not appear to other people to be anxious. Finally, a general lack of life satisfaction and a reduction in pleasure and happiness can also suggest that you would benefit from treatment. There are effective psychological and pharmacological treatments for social anxiety.

Some forms of help are available through self-help workbooks and Internet based treatments. There are a number of useful books that are widely available. We recommend two books on anxiety in the *Coping With* series to which our book contributes: *Coping with an Anxious or Depressed Child: A Guide for Parents and Carers* by Sam Cartwright-Hatton, published in 2007, and *Coping with Fears and Phobias: A Step-by-Step Guide to Understanding and Facing Your Anxieties* by Warren Mansell, published in 2007. Another useful workbook is *Overcoming Social Anxiety: A Self-Help Guide Using Cognitive Behavioural Techniques* by Gillian Butler, published in 1999. As the title suggests, her approach includes exercises based on cognitive behaviour therapy. There are several Internet sites that offer advice to people suffering from shyness, social anxiety and problems with blushing. We gave examples of some of these in chapters 6 and 9, and we list their website addresses in the appendix. The sites provide useful information about these anxieties and some of them can put you in contact with self-help groups or help you to find therapists. These sources of help are valuable, particularly if your circumstances mean that you are isolated from alternative forms of help. However, one of the messages that we wish to convey is that it is very difficult to overcome your anxiety just by reading about it. We hope that our book is informative about the nature of social anxiety and the forms of intervention that are available, and will give you leads that you follow up. If you decide after reading it that you would benefit from help we have suggested ways of choosing it. Overcoming anxiety requires following a programme of action. The programme of action must be structured in order to be effective. It is very difficult to do this by yourself, to have the motivation to initiate and continue with activities. Feedback and encouragement from others is also very important.

## Cognitive behavioural therapy

The most widely investigated psychological treatment programmes are based on cognitive behavioural therapy. Research shows that CBT is effective for social anxiety. CBT emphasizes the importance of a collaborative relationship between the therapist and patient or client, the need to arrive at a clear understanding of the patient's situation, and encouragement to take an alternative perspective on the patient's problems. As we have seen, it emphasizes the role of thinking in the maintenance of social anxiety. It addresses two aspects of thinking: the content of thoughts – what you are thinking about – and thought process, how you arrive at judgements and conclusions about social events. This process can be automatic, taking place without full awareness. It can lead to problems if it causes you to jump to conclusions based on past experiences rather than present events – conclusions that are not based on the thoughtful appraisal that you might, for example, apply to other people's anxieties.

Clinical research and practice have found that people with SAD have several types of self-damaging cognitions, including negative beliefs about themselves and others, negatively biased predictions for social events, inaccurate judgements during social events, and the tendency to dwell on things long after the event has passed. Negative beliefs lead to feelings of anxiety even before you enter a social situation. Anxiety results in self-consciousness, which is an unpleasant experience in itself and which makes effective and satisfying interactions with others more difficult. It also encourages the adoption of safety behaviours. We have drawn attention to the negative consequences of these behaviours throughout the book. They don't deliver what they seem to promise and they make things more difficult in the longer run.

Cognitive behaviour therapy aims to change these processes. As we saw in chapters 7 and 8, it includes a number of components:

- Increase patients' understanding of social anxiety disorder. Therapists do this by presenting a model that summarizes what is known about social anxiety and by encouraging patients to apply this model to their experiences.
- Increase patients' awareness of the nature of interpersonal behaviours and social relationships.
- Develop patients' ability to monitor their behaviour to become aware how social anxiety works in their life.
- Help patients to develop a personal model that describes the cognitive and behavioural processes that contribute to their social anxiety.
- Help patients to participate in structured behavioural exercises to evaluate the accuracy of negative beliefs and predictions.
- Help patients carry out behavioural experiments where they change their behaviour in a systematic way and observe the results. These can help the patient evaluate safety behaviours.
- Help patients to carry out behavioural experiments where they deliberately engage in feared behaviours in order to evaluate whether such behaviours as trembling, pausing, or stammering inevitably lead to negative social outcomes.

- Teach patients to carry out observations of other people in order to evaluate the accuracy of their negative beliefs.
- Encourage patients to learn how to place any negative social outcomes that do occur in a broader perspective.

## Medication

Pharmacological treatments are available for social anxiety disorder. Selective Serotonin Reuptake Inhibitors (SSRIs) are the most widely used medication in the treatment of generalized social anxiety disorder. There is controversy in the clinical literature about whether research evidence shows convincingly that SSRIs are effective in the treatment of depression and anxiety disorders. While some research studies have concluded that there is little evidence that they are effective, pharmaceutical companies argue that clinical experience shows that they are effective. There is also concern about their suitability for all patients. Specifically, there is concern about their possible side effects, particularly the possibility of greater likelihood of suicidal thinking among young people taking them. Clinical guidelines are that patients should try psychological forms of treatment before SSRIs should be prescribed. Your doctor should be approached on this issue if you think medication might help you. We have argued that it is essential that the patient works closely with their doctor through all stages of medication. There can be side effects, interactions with other medications or with elements in the patient's health or diet, and individual patients can experience problems with specific drugs. Patients should not continue if there are side effects, switch from one medication to another, or cease taking medicines without full discussion with their doctor. They should draw the doctor's attention to life changes that might impact on their behaviour or on taking medication.

A number of different SSRIs are available for SAD. Doctors may recommend changing from one SSRI to another in order to maximize effectiveness or to control any side effects. SSRIs are not interchangeable with other forms of medication such as MAOIs and a period of time has to elapse before the patient switches from one class of medication to the other. Chapter 9 gives further information about MAOIs and reversible MAOIs, which have also been applied to the treatment of social anxiety disorder.

Beta blockers have been widely applied to the treatment of anxiety symptoms. They are often prescribed for people suffering from specific performance anxieties, when the period during which anxiety is experienced can be specified. They are less useful when the period during which anxiety will be experienced is extended or uncertain. Benzodiazepines are widely used in the treatment of anxiety symptoms. The principal limitations of their use in social anxiety disorder are their possible adverse side effects and their potential for abuse and addiction. Beta blockers and Benzodiazepines are prescription-only drugs and should only be taken under medical supervision.

## Finally

We hope that this book will have proved of interest and value to you. If your reason for deciding to read it was to learn more about shyness and social anxiety in general or about social phobia or social anxiety disorder in particular, we hope that our book has gone some way to give you the information you sought. Your reason for reading it may be that your life, or the life of someone you know, is impaired by social anxiety or you believe that shyness or anxiety prevents you or them from fulfilling potential or having the social relationships and friendships that are longed for. We have aimed to explain to you what psychology knows about the nature of social anxiety and in particular about the recurrent thoughts and thinking processes that underlie anxiety. We have aimed to explain the various forms of treatment that are available to reduce anxiety. We set out details of cognitive behaviour therapy in some detail because evidence suggests that it is the most effective form of treatment that we currently have. Unfortunately there are serious problems of access to this. In 2008 the government announced additional resources available to shorten waiting times for cognitive therapy, but this may not reduce waiting lists appreciably in the immediate future given the high demand for treatment for depression, anxiety, and social anxiety disorder. However, it does indicate the seriousness with which anxiety problems are regarded and the value that is placed upon cognitive behaviour therapy for their treatment. It is hoped that access will improve and that the benefits of psychological therapy will continue to be demonstrated. Your doctor should be in a position to give you advice on how to access therapy. Some of the Internet sites we reviewed in chapter 6 give helpful information on the availability of therapists in specific regions.

Social anxiety can be a chronic condition that causes great distress; nevertheless distress can be reduced and anxiety can be overcome.

# Notes

## Chapter 1: Is this book for you?

The terms 'cognitive behaviour therapy' and 'cognitive behavioural therapy' are both in current use to refer to the same form of psychological therapy.

## Chapter 2: What is social anxiety?

p. 19. Alfred Hitchcock's *Vertigo*, made in 1958, is currently distributed by Universal Pictures and is available on DVD.

p. 23. For the Stanford Shyness Survey see Zimbardo, P. G. *Shyness: What It Is. What to Do about It*, Addison-Wesley, 1977.

See also: *The Shyness Home Page*, the website of the Shyness Institute, directed by Philip Zimbardo and Lynne Henderson. http://www.shyness.com

p. 24. National Comorbidity Survey. Findings are from Kessler, R. C., McGonagle, K. A., Zhao, S., Nelson, C. B., Hughes, M., Eshleman, S., Wittschen, H. -U., and Kendler, K. S. (1994). Lifetime and 12-month prevalence of DSM-III-R psychiatric disorders in the United States. *Archives of General Psychiatry*, 51, 8–19.

See also: Ingram, R. E., Ramel, W., Chavira, D., and Scher, C., Social anxiety and depression, in Crozier, W. R. and Alden, L. E. (eds), *The Essential Handbook of Social Anxiety for Clinicians*, Wiley, 2005, pp. 241–264.

p. 26. 'Competent Other'. See Scott, S. (2004). The shell, the stranger and the competent other: Towards a sociology of shyness. *Sociology*, vol. 38, no. 1, 121–137. Also see Dr Scott's shyness website at http://www.sussex.ac.uk/Users/ss216

## Chapter 3: What is shyness?

p. 31. See *The Gospel According to Chris Moyles*, Ebury Press, 2007, particularly pages 228 and 277. Also interview with Dominic Byrne on chrismoyles.net, http://chrismoyles.co.uk/phpBB3/viewtopic.php?t=16028

p. 32. Ella Fitzgerald. See, for example, *PBS American Masters* website, http://www.pbs.org/wnet/americanmasters/database/fitzgerald_e.html

p. 35. Alan Bennett, *Untold Stories*, London: Faber and Faber, 2005, pp. 43–44.

p. 36. 'Who does she think she is?' Crozier, W. R. and Garbert-Jones, A. (1996). Finding a voice. *Adults Learning*, vol. 7, no. 8, 195–198.

p. 37. For changes over recent years in shyness in China, see Chen, X., Cen, G., Li, D., and He, Y. (2005). Social functioning and adjustment in Chinese children: the imprint of historical time. *Child Development*, vol. 76, 182–195.

p. 38. Ban Ki-moon. See *The Sunday Times*, 8 October 2006, p. 21, or *The Real Truth*, 29 December 2006, http://www.realtruth.org/articles/515-bkusg.html

p. 39. For shyness in Finland see Berry, M., Carbaugh, D., and Nurmikari-Berry, M. (2004). Communicating Finnish quietude: a pedagogical process for discovering implicit cultural meanings in languages. *Language and Intercultural Communication*, vol. 4, 261–280.

p. 46. Statistics on girls' participation and discussion of the role of embarrassment in discouraging their participation in games lessons can be found in reports by the Equal Opportunities Commission (*Gender Equality Duty and Schools*), Youth Sport Trust and Women's Sports Foundation-East.

p. 48. 'man fearless in battle'. The quotations from Darwin come from his chapter on blushing in his book, *The Expression of Emotions in Man and Animals,* 1872. The text is available on the World Wide Web, for example: http://www.human nature.com/darwin/emotion/chap13.htm

## Chapter 4: The experience of shyness

p. 54. Benjamin Constant's *Adolphe* is published in English by Penguin Classics, 1980.

p. 56. 'Chronic niceness', see Rapson, J. and English, C., *Anxious to Please,* published by Sourcebooks, 2006.

p. 61. Stanford Survey: see notes for chapter 2.

p. 62. Box 1. For Adam Smith, Helen Block Lewis and self-consciousness, see Crozier, W. R. *Blushing and the Social Emotions,* Basingstoke: Palgrave Macmillan, 2006, pp. 32–36.

p. 64. Box 2. The questionnaire was designed by Professor Bernardo J. Carducci, who is Director of the Shyness Research Institute in Indiana University Southeast in the United States. His website contains additional information about the questionnaire as well as details of Dr Carducci's research. http://www.ius.edu/shyness

p. 66. Jerome Kagan; see Kagan, J. and Snidman, N., *The Long Shadow of Temperament,* The Belknap Press of Harvard University Press, 2004.

p. 70. Delayed marriage among shy men. See Caspi, A., Elder, G. H. Jr, and Bem, D. J. (1988). Moving away from the world: Life-course patterns of shy children. *Developmental Psychology,* 24, 824–831.

## Chapter 5: What is social anxiety disorder?

p. 76. American Psychiatric Association, *Diagnostic and Statistical Manual of Mental Disorders.* Fourth edition Text Revision, Washington, DC, 2000.

p. 84. For SPIN see Connor, K. M., Davidson, J. R. T., Churchill, L. E., Sherwood, A., Foa, E. B., and Weisler, R. H. (2000). Psychometric properties of the Social Phobia Inventory (SPIN): a new self-rating scale. *British Journal of Psychiatry*, 176, 379–386.

p. 88. 'one study estimated that only three per cent of diagnosed cases had received treatment within the preceding year'. See Davidson, J. R. T., Hughes, D. L., George, L. K., and Blazer, D. G. (1993). The epidemiology of social phobia: Findings from the Duke Epidemiological Catchment Area Study. *Psychological Medicine*, 23, 709–718.

p. 88. 'It is a chronic disorder.' See Ingram, R. E., Ramel, W., Chavira, D., and Scher, C., Social anxiety and depression, op. cit.

p. 89. Bernardo J. Carducci. See Carducci, B. J., What shy individuals do to cope with their shyness: a content analysis, in Crozier, W. R. (ed.), *Shyness: Development, Consolidation and Change*, Routledge, 2000, pp. 171–185.

p. 90. Social anxiety in children: See Rapee, R. M., and Sweeney, L., Social phobia in children and adolescents, in Crozier, W. R. and Alden, L. E. (eds), *The Essential Handbook of Social Anxiety for Clinicians*, Wiley, 2005, pp. 123–151.

## Chapter 6: Is treatment for you?

pp. 96–102. Schneier and his colleagues have evaluated how social anxiety affects life functioning: Schneier, F. R., Heckelman, L. R., Garfinkel, R., Campeas, R., Fallon, B. A., Gitow, A., Street, L., Del Bene, D., and Liebowitz, M. R. (1994). Functional impairment in social phobia. *Journal of Clinical Psychiatry*, 55, 322–331.

p. 99. For a discussion of school-based treatment programmes for social anxiety in children, see McLoone, J., Hudson, J. L., and Rapee, R. M. (2006). Treating anxiety disorders in a school setting. *Education & Treatment of Children*, 29, 219–242.

p. 100. Survey research indicates that social phobia can impair workplace performance. For example, Stein, M.B., Torgrud, L.J., and Walker, J.R. (2000). Social phobia symptoms, subtypes, and severity: findings from a community survey. *Archives of General Psychiatry*, 57, 1046–1052.

p. 103. For a discussion of the effects of social anxiety on positive emotions: Kashdan, T. B. (2004). The neglected relationship between social interaction anxiety and hedonic deficits: Differentiation from depressive symptoms. *Journal of Anxiety Disorders*, 18, 719–730.

p. 103. Sonja Lyubomirsky has conducted a number of groundbreaking studies of the factors that lead to happiness, including the role of social interactions in positive affect. Tkach, C. and Lyubomirsky, S. (2006). How do people pursue happiness? Relating personality, happiness-increasing strategies, and well-being. *Journal of Happiness Studies*, 7, 183–225.

p. 103. Lyubomirsky, S., King, L., and Diener, E. (2005). The benefits of frequent positive affect: Does happiness lead to success? *Psychological Bulletin*, 131, 803–855.

p. 109. Paul Emmelkamp has conducted a comparison between CBT and dynamic therapies for social avoidance. See Emmelkamp, P. M. G., Benner, A., Kuipers, A., Feiertag, G. A., Koster, H.C., and van Apeldoorn, F.J. (2006). Comparison of brief dynamic and cognitive-behavioural therapies in avoidant personality disorder. *British Journal of Psychiatry*, 189, 60–64.

p. 110. Ron Rapee conducted a scientific evaluation of the effectiveness of self-help books. See Rapee, R. M., Abbott, M. J., and Baillie, A. M. (2007). Treatment of social phobia through pure self-help and therapist-augmented self-help. *British Journal of Psychiatry*, 191, 246–252.

p. 117. For a comparison of CBT, pharmacotherapy, and a combination of the two treatments, see Davidson, J. R. T., Foa, E. B., and Huppert, J. D. (2004). Fluoxetine, comprehensive cognitive behavioral therapy, and placebo in generalized social phobia. *Archives of General Psychiatry*, 61, 1005–1013.

p. 117. A detailed description of group CBT can be found in Heimberg, R. G. and Becker, R. E., *Cognitive-Behavioral Group Therapy for Social Phobia: Basic Mechanisms and Clinical Strategies*, Guilford Press, 2002.

p. 118. Sherry Stewart and her colleagues conducted a number of studies on the association of social anxiety and alcohol use and abuse. See Morris, E. P., Stewart, S. H., and Ham, L. S., (2005). The relationship between social anxiety disorder and alcohol use disorders: A critical review. *Clinical Psychology Review*, 25, 734–760.

p. 119. For the benefits of increasing activity levels for improving mood, see Cartwright-Hatton, S., *Coping with an Anxious or Depressed Child*, Oneworld Publications, 2007, pp. 54–55.

## Chapter 7: Psychological therapy

pp. 124–133. The predominant clinical theories of social phobia emphasize the role of cognitive processes. See the following references for summaries of these theories.

Beck, A. T., Emery, G., and Greenberg, R., *Anxiety Disorders and Phobias: A Cognitive Perspective*, Basic Books, 1985.

Clark, D. M., A cognitive perspective on social phobia, in Crozier, W. R. and Alden, L. E. (eds), *International Handbook of Social Anxiety: Concepts, Research and Interventions Relating to the Self and Shyness*, Wiley, 2001, pp. 405–430.

Clark, D. M. and Wells, A., A cognitive model of social phobia, in Heimberg, R. G., Liebowitz, M., Hope, D. and Schneier, F. R. (eds), *Social Phobia: Diagnosis, Assessment, and Treatment*, Guilford Press, 1995, pp. 69–93.

Rapee, R. M. and Heimberg, R. G. (1997). A cognitive behavioural model of anxiety in social phobia. *Behaviour Research and Therapy*, 35, 741–756.

p. 127. Research suggests that socially anxious people overestimate the likelihood and cost of negative social outcomes. See, for example: Foa, E. B., Franklin, M. E., Perry, K. J., and Herbert, J. D. (1996). Cognitive biases in generalized social phobia. *Journal of Abnormal Psychology*, 105, 433–439.

p. 127. Changes in overestimations of the likelihood and cost of negative social outcomes are important to improvement. See Hofmann, S. G. (2004). Cognitive mediation of treatment change in social phobia. *Journal of Consulting and Clinical Psychology*, 72, 392–399.

p. 131. Over-agreeableness. See also note for chronic niceness (chapter 4, p. 56).

pp. 135–143. This model is discussed in detail by David M. Clark (2001) op. cit.

pp. 137–140. A description of self-monitoring can be found in Antony, M. and Rowa, A., *Social Anxiety Disorder*, Hogrefe & Huber, 2005.

## Chapter 8: Overcoming social anxiety: strategies for change

pp. 146–159. A detailed description of how to conduct behavioural experiments is provided in Bennett-Levy, J., Butler, G., Fennell, M., Hackmann, A., Mueller, M., and Westbrook, D. (eds), *Oxford Guide to Behavioural Experiments in Cognitive Therapy*, Oxford University Press, 2004.

pp. 156–161. The role of interpersonal relationships in social anxiety disorder is summarized in Alden, L. E. and Taylor, C. T. (2004). Interpersonal perspectives on social phobia. *Clinical Psychology Review*, 24, 857–882.

p. 160. The way in which openness influences liking is discussed in Collins, N. L. and Miller, L. C. (1994). Self-disclosure and liking: A meta-analytic review. *Psychological Bulletin*, 116, 457–475.

pp. 163–164. Several well-designed research studies provide support for the effectiveness of CBT. A treatment study conducted in the UK can be found in Clark, D. M., Ehlers, A., Hackmann, A., McManus, F., Fennell, M., Grey, N., et al. (2006). Cognitive therapy versus exposure and applied relaxation in social phobia: A randomized controlled trial. *Journal of Consulting and Clinical Psychology*, 74, 568–578.

pp. 163–164. Group CBT has also been shown to be effective in overcoming social anxiety symptoms. See Heimberg, R. G., Liebowitz, M. R., Hope, D. A., Scheier, F. R., Holt, C. S., Welkowitz, L. A., et al. (1998). Cognitive behavioral group therapy versus phenelzine therapy for social phobia: 12-week outcome. *Archives of General Psychiatry*, 55, 1133–1141.

p. 164. Some studies have followed up patients who received CBT for their social anxiety. These studies indicate that treatment gains are maintained over time. See Clark, D. M., Ehlers, A., Hackmann, A., McManus, F., Fennell, M., Grey, N., et al. (2006). Cognitive therapy versus exposure and applied relaxation in social phobia: A randomized controlled trial. *Journal of Consulting and Clinical Psychology*, 74, 568–578.

p. 164. For a review of the effectiveness of CBT for social anxiety disorder, see Rodebaugh, T. L., Holaway, R. M., and Heimberg, R. G. (2004). The treatment of social anxiety disorder. *Clinical Psychology Review*, 24, 883–908.

## Chapter 9: Medication

p. 168. Box 1. National Institute for Health and Clinical Excellence (2007). *Quick Reference Guide (amended). Anxiety: managements of anxiety (panic disorder, with or without agoraphobia, and generalized anxiety disorder) in adults in primary, secondary and community care. Clinical Guideline 22 (amended).* London: National Institute for Clinical Excellence. http://www.nice.org.uk/CG022

p. 172. Box 2. For an accessible account of neurotransmitters, see O'Shea, M., *The Brain: A Very Short Introduction*, Oxford University Press, 2005, chapter 3.

p. 175. Box 3. Medicine and Healthcare products Regulatory Agency (2003). *Report of the CSM Expert Working Group on the safety of Selective Serotonin Reuptake Inhibitor Antidepressants.* http://www.mhra.gov.uk/home/groups/plp/documents/drugsaf etymessage/con019472.pdf

p. 183. 'Research has shown.' For a review of research studies, see Hood, S. D. and Nutt, D. J., Psychopharmacological treatments: an overview, in Crozier, W. R. and Alden, L. E. (eds), *The Essential Handbook of Social Anxiety for Clinicians*, Wiley, 2005, pp. 287–320.

p. 183. Liebowitz Social Anxiety scale. See Heimberg, R. G., Horner, K. J., Juster, H. R., Safren, S. A., Brown, E. J., Schneier, F. R., and Liebowitz, M. R. (1999). Psychometric properties of the Liebowitz Social Anxiety Scale. *Psychological Medicine*, 29, 199–212. The website of the Social Anxiety Research Clinic (http://asp.cumc. columbia.edu/SAD/Survey_main.asp) has information about the scale and about the Anxiety Disorders Clinic located at the New York State Psychiatric Institute at Columbia University Medical Center, New York. See also the Adult Anxiety Clinic of Temple University for information about the social anxiety treatment, research and training programme at this clinic based in Temple University, Pennsylvania, USA (http://www.temple.edu/phobia).

p. 185. National Institute for Clinical Excellence (2004). *Depression: Management of depression in primary and secondary care. Clinical practice guideline No. 23*. London: National Institute for Clinical Excellence. http://www.nice.org.uk/CG023

p. 186. Box 4. Kirsch, I., et al. (2008). Initial severity and antidepressant benefits: A meta-analysis of data submitted to the Food and Drug Administration, *PLOS Medicine*, 5, 2, e45. http://www. plosmedicine.org

p. 188. Box 5. Furmark, T., Tillfors, M., Garpenstrand, H., Marteinsdottir, I., Långström, B., Oreland, L., and Frederikson, M. (2004). Serotonin transporter polymorphism related to amygdala excitability and symptom severity in patients with social phobia. *Neuroscience Letters*, 362, 189–192.

p. 188. For discussion of the effects of psychological treatment on brain functioning, see Kumari, V. (2006). Do psychotherapies produce neurobiological effects? *Acta Neuropsychiatrica*, 18, 61–70.

p. 190. For a critical evaluation of studies of the brain and social phobia, see Stravynski, A., *Fearing Others: The Nature and Treatment of Social Phobia*, Cambridge University Press, 2007, chapter 6.

p. 191. Nick Clegg's speech was reported in the *Guardian*, 8 February 2008, p. 16.

p. 191. The British government announced initiatives in July 2007 that are intended to speed up access to cognitive behaviour therapy. In February 2008, the Health Secretary followed up this initiative and announced plans for investment in a major programme.

p. 192. It is not uncommon for drugs developed for treatment for one condition to be found to be effective for another. Chlorpromazine, which has been widely used in the treatment of schizophrenia, was developed to reduce the effect of shock in surgery. In 2007 there were claims that medication used for arthritis can be effective in alleviating symptoms of Alzheimer's disease, although this has not yet been submitted to rigorous scientific evaluation.

## Chapter 10: Fear of blushing

p. 197. Fear of blushing and diagnostic criteria for social phobia. The study was reported in Gerlach, A. L. and Ultes, M., Überschneidung von Socializer Phobie und ubermässigem Schwitzen und Erröten – eine internetbasierte Studie, in Ott, R. and Eichenberg, C. (eds), *Klinische Psychologie im Internet*, Hogrefe Verlag, 2003, pp. 327–341. See Crozier, op. cit, pp. 194–195.

p. 197. Box 1. Ishiyama, F. I. (1984). Shyness: Anxious social sensitivity and self-isolating tendency. *Adolescence*, 19, 903–911.

p. 198. Blushing as a symptom of social anxiety. See Amies, P. L., Gelder, M. G., and Shaw, P. M. (1983). Social phobia: a comparative case study. *British Journal of Psychiatry*, 142, 174–179.

p. 201. For Darwin, see notes for chapter 3.

p. 204. See Cutlip, W. D. and Leary, M. R. (1993). Anatomic and physiological bases of social blushing: Speculations from neurology and psychology. *Behavioural Neurology*, 6, 181–185, p. 183.

p. 205. For exposure and the blush, see also Daniel C. Dennett, The Computational Perspective: A talk with Daniel C. Dennett, *Edge*, 19 November 2001, http://www.edge.org/3rd_culture/dennett2/dennett2_p4.html

p. 205. 'I don't know what things are good to do . . .' Harkins, J. (1990). Shame and shyness in the Aboriginal classroom: A case for 'practical semantics'. *Australian Journal of Linguistics*, 10, 293–306. Reprinted by permission of the publisher, Taylor & Francis Ltd, http://www.tandf.co.uk/journals

p. 208. Complexion and blushing. See Crozier, op. cit, p. 171.

p. 209. Box 3. Mulkens, S., de Jong, P. J., and Bögels, S. M. (1997). High blushing propensity: Fearful preoccupation or facial coloration? *Personality and Individual Differences*, 22, 817–824.

p. 214. Box 4. Drott, C., Claes, G., Olsson-Rex, L., Dalman, P., Fahlén, T., and Göthberg, G. (1998). Successful treatment of facial blushing by endoscopic transthoracic sympathicotomy. *British Journal of Dermatology*, 138, 639–643.

## Chapter 11: Rounding things up

p. 224. Butler, G., *Overcoming Social Anxiety: A Self-help Guide Using Cognitive Behavioural Techniques*, Robinson Publishing, 1999.

Cartwright-Hatton, S., *Coping with an Anxious or Depressed Child: A Guide for Parents and Cavers*, Oneworld Publications, 2007.

Mansell, W., *Coping with Fears and Phobias: A Step-by-Step Guide to Understanding and Facing your Anxieties*, Oneworld Publications, 2007.

# Appendix

## List of websites and their contact addresses

### Chapter 2: What is social anxiety?

| | |
|---|---|
| The Shyness Institute | http://www.shyness.com |
| Dr Susie Scott's shyness website | http://www.sussex.ac.uk/Users/ss216 |

### Chapter 4: The experience of shyness

| | |
|---|---|
| Dr Carducci's shyness website | http://www.ius.edu/shyness |

### Chapter 6: Is treatment for you?

| | |
|---|---|
| Anxiety Disorders Association of America | http://www.adaa.org |
| Anxiety UK | http://www.anxietyuk.org.uk |
| The British Association for Behavioural and Cognitive Psychotherapy | http://www.babcp.com/search/therapsit.asp |
| The British Psychological Society | http://www.bps.org.uk |

No Panic                                http://www.nopanic.org.uk

Social Anxiety UK (SA-UK)               http://www.social-anxiety.org.uk

## Chapter 9: Medication

Adult Anxiety Clinic of Temple          http://www.temple.edu/phobia

University Anxiety Disorders            http://asp.cumc.columbia.edu/
Clinic, Columbia University             SAD/Survey_main.asp

National Institute for Health           http://www.nice.org.uk/CG022
and Clinical Excellence

## Chapter 10: Fear of blushing

The Center for Hyperhidrosis            http://www.Sweaty-palms.com/
                                        blushing.html

ESFB Channel                            http://www.esfbchannel.com

ETS and Reversals Discussion            http://p069.ezboard.com/
Forum                                   betsandreversals

Patients Against                        http://ets-sideeffects.net/
Sympathectomy Surgery                   home3.3.1.html

Social Anxiety UK (SA-UK)               http://www.social-anxiety.org.
                                        uk/puce/

Swedish Support Group                   http://home.swipnet.se/
                                        sympatiska/sideeff.htm

# Index